ORTHO'S All About

Fences
and Gates

Written by Martin Miller

Meredith® Books
Des Moines, Iowa

Ortho® Books
An imprint of Meredith® Books

Ortho's All About Fences and Gates
Editor: Larry Johnston
Contributing Writer: Martin Miller
Art Director: Tom Wegner
Assistant Art Director: Harijs Priekulis
Copy Chief: Catherine Hamrick
Copy and Production Editor: Terri Fredrickson
Book Production Managers: Pam Kvitne,
    Marjorie J. Schenkelberg
Contributing Copy Editor: Steve Hallam
Technical Proofreader: Charles I. Hedlund
Contributing Proofreaders: Dan Degen, Fran Gardner,
    Colleen Johnson
Contributing Prop/Photo Stylist: Peggy Johnston
Indexer: Barbara L. Klein
Electronic Production Coordinator: Paula Forest
Editorial and Design Assistants: Kathleen Stevens,
    Karen Schirm

Additional Editorial Contributions from
    Art Rep Services
Director: Chip Nadeau
Designer: lk Design
Illustrator: Shawn Wallace

Meredith® Books
Editor in Chief: James D. Blume
Design Director: Matt Strelecki
Managing Editor: Gregory H. Kayko
Executive Ortho Editor: Larry Erickson

Director, Retail Sales and Marketing: Terry Unsworth
Director, Sales, Special Markets: Rita McMullen
Director, Sales, Premiums: Michael A. Peterson
Director, Sales, Retail: Tom Wierzbicki
Director, Sales, Home & Garden Centers: Ray Wolf
Director, Book Marketing: Brad Elmitt
Director, Operations: George A. Susral
Director, Production: Douglas M. Johnston

Vice President, General Manager: Jamie L. Martin

Meredith Publishing Group
President, Publishing Group: Christopher M. Little
Vice President, Finance & Administration: Max Runciman

Meredith Corporation
Chairman and Chief Executive Officer: William T. Kerr

Chairman of the Executive Committee: E.T. Meredith III

Thanks to
Mark and Tonya Swanda, Des Moines, Iowa
Daniel Morlan, Earl May Nursery and Garden Center,
    West Des Moines, Iowa
Western Wood Products Association

Photographers
    (Photographers credited may retain copyright ©
    to the listed photographs.)
L = Left, R = Right, C = Center, B = Bottom, T = Top
Baldwin Photography: front cover
Laurie Black: 6T, 39B; John Blaustein: 13B
Ernest Braun, California Redwood Association: 75B
Ernest Braun: 72; Gary Bumgarner: 13T
Josephine Coatsworth: 38B; Alan Copeland: 15L
Crandall & Crandall: 3C, 10B, 11B, 14T
Stephen Cridland: 73TR; George deGennaro: 8B
Susan Gilmore: 6B; Bob Greenspan: 4C
Inside Out Studio: 3B, 86T, 87T, 88B
Michael Jensen: 4T; Jim Kascoutas: 47TL, 47
Susan Lammers: 3T, 4BC, 4B
James McNair: 38; Douglas Muir: 15R; Z. Ode: 7T
Tom Rider, California Redwood Association: 10T, 74, 75T
Jeff Weissman, California Redwood Assoication: 11T, 11C

All of us at Ortho® Books are dedicated to providing you
with the information and ideas you need to enhance your
home and garden. We welcome your comments and
suggestions about this book. Write to us at:
    Meredith Corporation
    Ortho Books
    1716 Locust St.
    Des Moines, IA 50309–3023

If you would like more information on other Ortho
products, call 800-225-2883 or visit us at www.ortho.com

Note to the Readers: Due to differing conditions, tools,
and individual skills, Meredith Corporation assumes no
responsibility for any damages, injuries suffered, or losses
incurred as a result of following the information published
in this book. Before beginning any project, review the
instructions carefully, and if any doubts or questions remain,
consult local experts or authorities. Because codes and
regulations vary greatly, you always should check with
authorities to ensure that your project complies with all
applicable local codes and regulations. Always read and
observe all of the safety precautions provided by
manufacturers of any tools, equipment, or supplies,
and follow all accepted safety procedures.

FENCING FOR A PURPOSE 4

A SAMPLER OF FENCE DESIGN 14

PLANNING FENCES 38

BUILDING FENCES 46

BUILDING GATES 72

TOOLS AND MATERIALS 86

4

FENCING FOR A PURPOSE

Fences variously mark boundaries, provide security, increase privacy, or temper the environment. These fences show an ideal blend of function and aesthetics. You can build useful and attractive fences for your property, too.

Fences organize open space. From the split Kentucky rails that marked frontier property lines to the sturdy, attractive redwood or cedar privacy fence around a suburban backyard, fences have long been a standard fixture of the American scene.

Fences are simple structures. Building most calls only for common tools and basic carpentry skills. And by choosing a style and materials carefully, you can match a fence to almost any budget. Perhaps because of that simplicity, few other home-improvement projects offer as much aesthetic and functional value in return for your energy, time, and money.

Fences can be more than merely functional, too. The best ones do their jobs with style and grace, contributing to your landscape. A well-designed and carefully built fence practically becomes an integral part of the yard or an extension of your home's architecture.

Whether you want a fence like that or a purely functional one, this book will help you build it. Here you can peruse styles ranging from rustic to formal to find the one that fits your needs. And of course, we've included complete instructions that show you how to plan and build the fence yourself, as well as a lot of good information about the best materials for your project and the tools you'll need to do the job. We've also included some practical suggestions for altering construction details so you can customize your fence.

Fence-building tradition extends from the wilderness to the plains, from the back forty to backyard suburbia. The following pages show you how to join in that tradition.

INVENTORY YOUR FENCING NEEDS

Every fence, no matter what its style, has a job to do—perhaps several jobs at once. To build the right fence—or fences—in your yard, you must first be sure about what you want to accomplish with fencing. Start by making an inventory of fencing on your property. Later on, you'll need to make detailed drawings. A clipboard and a rough sketch will do for now.

Here's what fences can do for you.
- Define a border or special area.
- Increase security and protection.
- Maintain privacy.
- Abate wind and noise.

You may have already decided that you need a lot-line fence, but don't limit yourself to just that fence yet. Look for other areas that fencing could improve: things you'd like to hide from view, inside or outside your yard, or areas you'd like to accentuate. As you inspect your yard, sketch potential fencing locations.

Put issues of style aside for the moment. At each potential fence site, ask yourself what the purpose of the fence is. What problems should it solve?

Note the purposes of each fence and rank the possible fences in order of their importance. If you can't erect all of them at one time, start with the one that has the highest priority.

Mark out trial fence lines on the ground with rope or garden hose, then consider materials and style. Make sure the materials, size, and structure of each fence are up to the task you've identified. For example, wire-bound reed is great for hiding garbage cans, but it won't provide security at the edges of your lot. After choosing materials and style, make detailed drawings—they'll keep construction surprises to a minimum and that will make the project more enjoyable.

DEFINING SPACES

A gracefully curved fence defines different areas in this yard but doesn't isolate either, thanks to the open, gridded design. Painting the fence white complements the home's style.

Defining property boundaries is the original role of fencing. If that is *your* first priority, the style you choose will depend on whether you install a front-yard fence or a backyard fence.

FRONT-YARD FENCES

Front-yard fences traditionally define the extent of the property and provide some (but not complete) security. Front fences usually aren't required to provide much privacy; if anything, their role is to seem inviting. The best fences emphasize particular features of the house or landscape in a way that harmonizes with the overall style of the home and its neighborhood.

Front-yard fences are usually shorter than those around backyards—3 to 4 feet is typical—but you can sometimes produce a striking effect by building a taller or lower one. Or, a fence can carry the color of the house or a design feature into the yard.

Defining a space may only require erecting a low or open fence. Where security, privacy, or containment is not a priority, any of the rail fences will do nicely along the front edge of the yard. Rail fences—even those that look hand-hewn and rustic—go well with most architectural designs. To accent the boundary of your yard or to call attention to a corner planting bed, build a simple corner rail.

Picket and chain-link fences are common lot-line fences for homeowners who want more containment and security. So are ornamental metal fences. They keep children and animals from running through the yard and provide a small measure of additional security. But don't overlook any material suitable to installations 3 to 4 feet high.

BACKYARD FENCES

In backyards, boundary-line marking takes on a different look because a fence needs to function as a lot-line marker and provide security and privacy as well. In many neighborhoods, you won't need to be as concerned with neighborhood styles as in your front yard.

A board fence, in any of its numerous styles and variations, is the right choice for many backyards. Board fences work well to combine lot-line definition with security and privacy. So do paling, stake, and siding fences.

PINPOINT THE PROPERTY LINE

Before you build a fence along your lot line, make sure you know exactly where the line is—along its entire length and on all sides of your property. Locating the lot-line markers may take a little detective work.

Start by looking for metal spikes or stakes. They may be buried or might never have been put in. If they're not visible, use a rented metal detector to find them.

When you locate them, replace each one with a 2-foot length of 1-inch galvanized pipe driven to within 1 inch of grade. (This way, you can see them later and the mower blade won't hit them.) Locate all the stakes; don't assume your lot lines are laid out in straight lines or right angles. A misplaced fence section invites trouble with neighbors and could lead to legal action.

If you can't find the lot-line markers, hire a surveyor. It will cost a few hundred dollars, but you'll avoid conflict with your neighbors and save the additional money you might have to spend to defend a lawsuit.

This tall redwood fence provides privacy. Imaginative design—incorporating openings to hold potted plants—softens the effect.

Fences separate the patio from pathways around it to help make the most of this small area. A fenced cubicle at the end conceals a utility area.

CODES AND COVENANTS

Before you start your fence planning—or at least early in the process—visit your local government building department to find out about local regulations that govern fences. You're likely to run into one or more of the following:

■ Building Codes—Almost all communities establish local codes that govern how residential structures should be built. These codes set standards for safety regarding materials and construction methods. Some communities' building codes specify the materials that you can use to build residential fences.

■ Zoning Ordinances—Zoning ordinances govern the use of property and establish maximum heights for structures (including fences) as well as how far they can be located from other properties (a distance called the setback). In many communities, zoning laws may prohibit certain materials and fence heights at the setback line, but allow these same materials farther away from the property line.

■ Covenants and Deed Restrictions— Some communities and neighborhoods write restrictions into property deeds to maintain neighborhood property values or to preserve specific architectural and historical styles. Such covenants may limit fence materials and locations.

Most localities have appeal procedures for codes, ordinances, and covenants. These procedures won't guarantee you'll be granted an exception (a variance), but they will ensure that your concerns will be heard.

After you've researched the restrictions that will affect your fence, incorporate them into your planning.

Combine any of these materials with lattice or louver panels— either as infill, as a top panel, or both—to keep the fence from being too confining.

SEPARATING AREAS

Lot lines aren't the only boundaries that need definition. So do the interior regions of your yard. Fences can keep work areas from visually spilling into recreation areas; they can separate storage space from relaxation retreats, entertainment areas from garden plots.

Small versions of the rail fence, for example, will separate your garden from other areas of your yard; and if you build a low fence with benches, you'll make your gardening more convenient and comfortable. Low fences should be between 12 and 24 inches high.

Tall screens built from stakes, lattice, and other materials with open patterns hide what's unattractive—the garbage cans, for example, or an unsightly metal storage shed. (Or you can conceal such things behind a vine-covered trellis—a fence-like structure.)

Three- to four-foot lath or lattice panels can screen the garden in the winter and provide a year-round accent. Wire-bound slat fencing doesn't have to be permanent. Roll it and wire it to metal posts so it's out of the way during the planting and growing seasons. Unroll it in the winter.

CHECK WITH THE UTILITIES

Do you know what's under the ground you want to dig up or install a fence over? Perhaps it's your water line or telephone connection. If you're not sure of the location of all your utility lines—plumbing, water, electrical, telephone, gas, and TV cable—call each utility company. Most utility firms will flag the location of their lines at no cost. Leave the flags in until your planning is done, and be sure to mark the line locations on your property plat map. Be specific— include depths and exact distances from structures and other reference points.

This fence is a design feature in itself. It hides a utility area and offers a garden seat plus a cozy nook with a table for two.

CREATING SECURITY

A board-and-batten fence offers security with privacy, but a long expanse of solid fencing can overwhelm adjacent spaces.

Creating security is often assumed to be the building of a structure to keep things out, but it also means keeping things in—or both. And depending on the purpose of security fences, their construction and materials can vary widely.

KEEPING THINGS IN

If your primary goal is containing toddlers in a play area, chain-link or wire-mesh fence with a 2-inch opening are excellent materials. Both offer sufficient height (at least 4 feet) and continuous visibility, allowing parents to keep an eye on their children's play.

A toddler-proof fence will not necessarily keep older children from straying, however. Chain link especially will give children toe holds for climbing as they grow taller and more adventuresome.

SPECIFICATIONS FOR SECURITY

Don't be taken in by loopholes in your own security fence. Many urban residents find that the fence they built to keep out burglars offers intruders cover from neighbors' views once the fence is scaled or breached.

A good security fence permits adequate visibility from the outside (wrought iron, tubular steel, and chain link are good choices). It should also be high enough to discourage prowlers (5 feet is a minimum; 6 feet or more is better if the style of the fence will not be compromised), tough enough to resist break-ins (wood is adequate, metal is better), and difficult to climb (no surfaces for handholds or footholds).

DOG FENCE DETAILS

Before you install a dog fence, answer these questions:
■ How high can your dog jump?
■ How deep can your dog dig?
If your dog is a puppy, answer the questions based on its mature size.

Your fence should be at least a couple of inches higher than your pet can jump—as a general rule, 6 feet high for larger dogs and 4 feet high for smaller dogs—and buried 6 inches to discourage tunneling.

You can avoid the whole dimensional issue of a dog fence with electronic fencing. Sold as invisible dog fencing, these systems rely on a buried wire and a collar worn by the dog. When the dog strays beyond the border of the wire, the collar senses it and gives the dog a mild shock. If your dog is particularly nervous or aggressive, however, the shock may not deter it and you may find yourself looking at the two questions above.

Chain link and wire mesh are also effective for containing smaller pets (see "Dog Fence Details" *above*). And metal is a better material than wood because dogs can't gnaw or scratch through it.

Containing larger animals—such as horses—in rural areas requires wire, panel, or rail fencing that is not covered in this book. Consult a local agricultural extension agent for information about these fences.

KEEPING THINGS OUT

Fencing designed to keep children or pets in will usually also keep children or pets out.

Iron fence sections, heavy posts, and a dig-proof zone of stones and concrete rubble along the bottom keep these dogs contained.

SWIMMING POOL FENCES

Drowning is the second leading cause of accidental death of children under three years.

If you have a swimming pool, make sure that its fence won't let unattended children in. Build it so children can't climb over or under it, or slip through its infill.

The fence should allow clear visibility from the outside into the pool area—chain link, pickets, and clear acrylic are good choices. Tall, closely spaced ornamental metal fencing offers a stylish alternative that is very hard to climb.

Gates should be self-closing and self-latching, and their construction should match the safety requirements of the fencing.

Check with your local building department for code requirements in your area. They should contain measures at least as strict as those established for swimming pools by the American Fence Association and the U.S. Consumer Products Safety Commission. Don't overlook your spa or garden pond—many communities define these as installations that require a fenced enclosure.

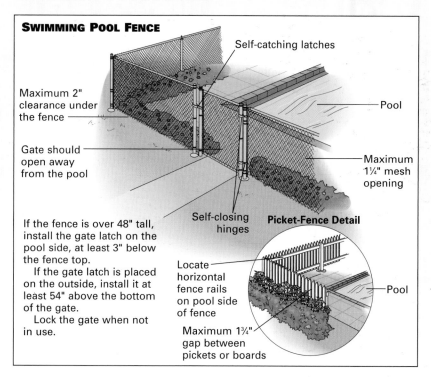

SWIMMING POOL FENCE

Self-catching latches

Maximum 2" clearance under the fence

Gate should open away from the pool

Pool

Maximum 1¼" mesh opening

If the fence is over 48" tall, install the gate latch on the pool side, at least 3" below the fence top.

If the gate latch is placed on the outside, install it at least 54" above the bottom of the gate.

Lock the gate when not in use.

Self-closing hinges

Picket-Fence Detail

Locate horizontal fence rails on pool side of fence

Pool

Maximum 1¾" gap between pickets or boards

If keeping intruders out is your priority, both the strength of your fence and its dimensions will change.

A security fence to keep out intruders should be tall, sturdy, and hard to climb. Although chain link often is used for security fencing, any of the solid-board or siding fence styles shown on pages 18 to 23 and 28 to 29 provide an additional psychological deterrent—they may prove more effective simply because intruders can't see what's on the other side.

Solid fences built primarily for security also provide complete privacy. But a secure enclosure comes with a price—it can feel confining.

To open the confinement, build see-through panels (small lattice windows, for example) in board or siding fencing. Use the panel framing shown on page 54 or modify some of the sections so they contain infill that isn't solid. Your design will be stylish and you'll avoid feeling like a prisoner of your own security project.

Before you finalize your security-fence design, research lighting and alarm systems. With motion-sensing lights and an alarm system that fits your lifestyle and budget, you can keep your property secure without having your fence as your only security feature.

FENCING OUT FOUR-LEGGED PESTS

Deer are lovely, graceful—and voracious. They usually have the same taste in flowers and landscape plantings that you do.

If your garden is small, a short fence may do the trick—deer, like the rest of us, don't like confined spaces. They don't like noise, either, so some small-plot gardeners have eliminated deer feeding by tying plastic grocery bags to rope or wire strung between posts. No matter what you do, clear tall brush and weeds away from the perimeter of your garden fence.

The most effective way to keep deer out is to build something they're not hungry enough to jump over. A 5-foot fence will hold back deer looking for a snack, but if deer food in the wild is in short supply, nothing less than 8 feet will do. If stylishness isn't necessary but economy is, string 4-inch woven wire or poultry wire between metal T-posts.

The smaller wire mesh will also keep out burrowing pests. Space the posts (use 4×4s at the corners) 10 feet apart, wire the fencing to the posts, and stake or bury the bottom.

INCREASING PRIVACY

Passersby can't see what's going on behind this redwood fence. The brick gate pillars enhance the solid look.

Of all the reasons for building a fence, establishing privacy is most often ranked highest by landscape architects. That's because we know we'll use our yard more often and our enjoyment of it will increase if we're not on display.

If you find yourself waving at your neighbors every time you're out in your own backyard, it's a sure sign that one or both of you should start planning for privacy.

SOLID FENCES, TOTAL PRIVACY

Creating privacy means blocking views. For privacy that's immediate and total, erect a tall wooden fence. Such fences are typically about 6 feet high (many communities prohibit fences that are higher). Consider the board fences shown later in this chapter, siding fences, paling fences, and slats. A basket-weave fence functions well as a privacy screen and offers some protection from the wind.

Be careful of fencing that provides total privacy, however. Solid fences have drawbacks. Over long distances, they tend to be imposing and confining—especially in narrow city yards. Also, if they're tall enough to provide the privacy you want, they may also cast total shade where you need dappled shade or no shade at all.

Tall, solid fences will also create strong downdrafts instead of blocking the wind. And although they provide privacy, they do so by obstructing the views beyond.

To solve these problems, you might not need solid fencing along the entire lot line. Study—from the point from which you will be observed—the patio or other area in which you need privacy. One bay of solid fencing that blocks the neighbors' angle of view may be all you need. To create privacy in a single section of a fence that runs the length of your lot-line, build tall sections where you want total privacy and short sections where you want to preserve the view. Or you can install lattice sections (or clear materials, such as acrylic) in the solid infill to let the views in

CONTROLLING NOISE WITH FENCES

Noise is as much of an intrusion on your privacy as are peering eyes. When it comes to noise control, the general rule is that the thicker and more dense the material, the more effective it is in muffling sound.

Solid masonry walls are perhaps the best structures to install if noise control is your greatest landscaping need. A wall is expensive, however, and may not be in keeping with your overall landscape design or your budget.

Don't expect solid board or board-on-board fences to do the job; their flat, hard surfaces don't absorb much sound. You can improve their effectiveness, however, by planting shrubs, vines, or other vegetation.

Board-and-batten and featherboard fences are more effective. Their surfaces have irregular planes that break up the sound waves and scatter them.

Plywood and tongue-and-groove fences are slightly better, but high shingle and clapboard fences will do the best job. These fences are built over an enclosure that acts as an air chamber that absorbs some of the sound, while the shingle or clapboard surface deflects it.

This rustic grape-stake panel is placed strategically to block neighbors' views.

where privacy is not needed. Such variations allow the fence (and you) to breathe.

LOUVERS AND LATTICE

Vertical louvers and lattice can be the perfect privacy fences because they screen views from the outside without creating a feeling of confinement.

These fences break up the lines of sight, calling attention to themselves without completely blocking the views beyond. You get privacy without complete obstruction and without feeling you're hemmed in by a stockade.

It's true you can see through vertical louvers or lattice, but usually not well enough to see what's going on behind the fence, since the eye usually focuses on the solid surfaces. (In front yards, however, the privacy potential of vertical louvers breaks down. Passengers in automobiles passing by at just the right speed can see right through the fence.) Horizontal louvers will block out views entirely.

PRIVACY BY DEGREE

Although it's usual to think of privacy in terms limited to completely blocking views, don't stop there. Just as rooms in the interior of your home have different privacy levels, so can different areas in your landscape.

A louvered redwood fence lets breezes through as it screens the view from this patio. Viewed from a slightly different angle (inset), the louvers afford little privacy.

You may need a tall fence to make a courtyard or patio private, but 4-foot bamboo or open-faced grapestake sections will more subtly seclude a backyard retreat. A 6-foot stockade may be fine for the perimeter of your yard, but low lattice panels with meandering morning glories will screen a utility area.

Lattice also works nicely overhead. Supported by posts and laced with vines, it will block views from above—perfect for tight-fitting urban yards with neighboring apartments or multistory structures.

FENCING SLOPES AND OBSTACLES

Don't let slopes and obstacles (trees, rocks, gullies, and banks) get in the way of your fencing plans. Make them part of your design.

You can remove trees, of course, but removal is costly and disruptive. Besides, it's not your only option. Build a curved fence portion around the tree (see pages 49 and 59) or if that won't work, stop the fence on one side of the tree and start it on the other (see page 45).

The same holds true for large rocks; they are often part of Mother Nature's original landscape design and they can become an important accent with construction techniques that highlight them. If your fence runs along the back edge of one of these accents of nature, change the infill material (or its pattern) behind the rock to show it off.

You can fill a recess in grade by extending the infill down to just above grade level, but building fences next to banks, steep slopes, and cliffs is more complicated. Consult a landscape architect to see whether you'll need to build a retaining wall— not the kind of incorporation into the landscape you want— to keep your fence from eventually washing away.

Decorative lattice panels break up the broad expanse of this fence line.

TEMPERING THE ENVIRONMENT

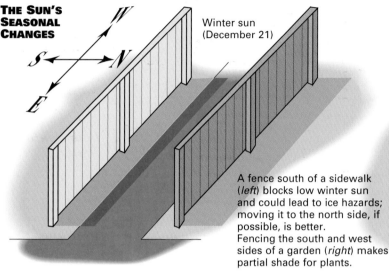

THE SUN'S SEASONAL CHANGES

Winter sun
(December 21)

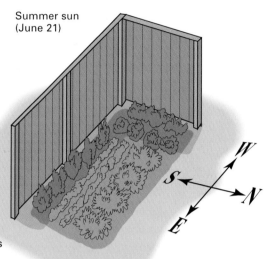

Summer sun
(June 21)

A fence south of a sidewalk (*left*) blocks low winter sun and could lead to ice hazards; moving it to the north side, if possible, is better.
Fencing the south and west sides of a garden (*right*) makes partial shade for plants.

Fences make your landscape much more comfortable and enjoyable. They provide shade, help light up dark areas, and reduce strong winds to gentle breezes.

As you conduct your inventory of fencing needs, take into account sun and wind patterns in your yard; identify areas that could use protection. Note those places on your sketches.

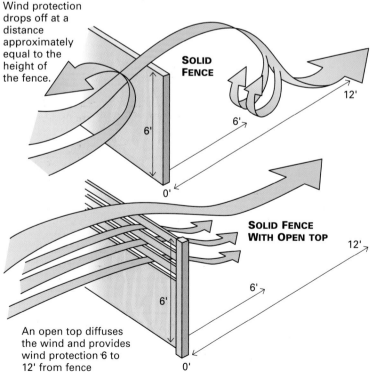

WINDSCREEN/FENCE HEIGHTS

Wind protection drops off at a distance approximately equal to the height of the fence.

SOLID FENCE

6'

6'

12'

0'

SOLID FENCE WITH OPEN TOP

6'

6'

12'

An open top diffuses the wind and provides wind protection 6 to 12' from fence

0'

STUDY FIRST, BUILD LATER

Your yard is full of microclimates—small areas where the temperature, sun patterns, and wind velocities differ from general conditions in your yard.

If you want fencing to increase shade, plot the course of the sun across your yard. Stake out shade patterns at different times of the day. Remember that the angle of the sun changes with the seasons. The winter sun is low in the southern horizon, so it casts shadows during much of the day. In the summer, shade can all but disappear from 10 a.m. to 3 p.m.

Include prevailing winds as well as seasonal breezes in your wind study. Prevailing winds blow from the same general direction over your region. Seasonal breezes are more localized and occur only at specific times of the day, intermittently during a season. Streamers tied to stakes will help reveal changing wind currents in your yard.

FENCING WITH THE SUN

The amount of shade a fence creates depends on its height, its proximity to the shaded area, and its axis. Tall, solid fencing can shade nearby decks, patios, or garden plots with special plantings that require only partial shade. Lattice panels make dappled shade; acrylic panels will let in all the sunlight. If you need constant shade throughout the year on the north side, build the fence on an east-west axis.

Fences will reflect light, too. If you paint the sunlit side of your fence with a light color,

This clever combination of louvers and lattice moderates the wind and affords privacy without seeming constrictive. The weathered wood lends a natural look, helping the fence to become an element of the landscape.

sunlight (and heat) will bounce into a nearby planting bed—a useful tool for gardeners whose spring plantings might be ruined by a late frost. A fence built to improve privacy will send warm light into a nearby south-facing room if you paint it a light color.

CONTROLLING THE WIND

Wind—like water—takes the path of least resistance. It spills over objects and creates microconditions in your landscape. Fences can adjust these conditions to your benefit.

For example, wind that blows across a patio surface and into the corner of the house creates eddies that swirl and dump debris before they move on. Control the prevailing wind to minimize the effect of those eddies,

but don't expect a solid fence to help much. Wind-control research shows that wind swirls over the top of solid objects and drops back down at a distance roughly equal to the height of the fence. (See the illustration on page 12.) Solid fences create low-pressure pockets that pull the wind down into the area you want protected.

Fences that divert or break up the wind provide better wind control. A louvered fence changes the direction of the wind and mitigates the debris-filled eddies noted above.

The open surface of board-on-board fences, grape-stake and spaced slats, and basket-weave and lattice fencing filters the wind and lets it through in a pleasant breeze instead of causing it to vault over the fence and come down with turbulence.

The playful pattern of this stained fence is designed not only for interest. It also softens the wind coming from the neighboring yard.

SNOW FENCE

Snow-fence design—the object of substantial research over the last 30 years—has become a science in itself. Here are the three types:

■ Plastic snow fence—Introduced in the 1960s, plastic snow fence is effective at containing snow. It has a serviceable life span of five years (longer if taken down between seasons) but requires considerable maintenance.

■ Lath fence—Also called Canadian or "cribbed" fence, it's made of 1½-inch lath wired in 25- or 50-foot rolls. It's longer-lived but not as effective as plastic or Wyoming snow fence.

■ Wyoming snow fence—Made of 1×6s spaced 6 inches apart, starting 10 inches above the ground, Wyoming snow fence will last 25 years or more, is as effective as plastic, and requires minimum maintenance.

Snow fence should run in a straight line, parallel to and centered on the area that you want to protect. It's best to orient it perpendicular to the prevailing winds and at a distance from the protected area equal to roughly 30 times its height.

A SAMPLER
OF FENCE DESIGN

The best fence fits easily into its surroundings as it serves its purpose. Planned and built carefully, a fence becomes an asset.

Armed with a sketch of your property and a clear notion of the job your fence or fences will do, you're ready to decide on style and design. You need an attractive style that satisfies the purposes for which you're building the fence.

Consider aesthetics from the broadest perspective—the established character of your home and neighborhood. Select fencing that harmonizes with established elements.

Look at other fences in the area. In a neighborhood of low rail fences, a tall stockade fence will look jarring and out of place. It could

Ornate post caps and a combination of tall and short pickets give this fence strong style.

Even an informal fence requires careful planning for location, size, color, and style. This variation of a Kentucky rail fence, painted crisp white, contrasts nicely with its setting.

lead to neighborhood tension, too. A shorter louvered fence might give the privacy you want while preserving neighborhood harmony.

Put up fencing that relates to your home's architecture, too. A 4-foot picket or ornamental iron fence will look better than rustic split rail or basketweave in front of a Victorian house.

As you look through the fence designs on the following pages, keep these ideas in mind:

Compatibility: Choose fence designs and materials that blend with neighborhood styles, the architecture of your house, streetscape elements, and your landscape.

Scale: Size the fence so it fits its function and location.

Proportion: Fences look awkward if their elements are out of balance. For example, a solid fence with lattice at the top looks right because the heavier element is on the bottom. Reversing the elements will make the fence seem top-heavy.

Cost: Length, height, design details, and material will all affect the cost of your fence. Consider, too, long-term maintenance cost. Always buy the highest quality materials you can afford.

And, if you like a style that's not quite right for your site or tastes, perhaps a slight modification will perfect it. A minor structural variation can make a big difference in a fence's appearance, so we've sprinkled design variations throughout this chapter.

Don't be afraid to experiment. Sketch out variations on paper. Creating a custom design can be as much fun as enjoying the benefits of the completed job.

DESIGN PROS

There are times when you need more advice to make a decision—especially if your fencing project is part of an overall landscape renovation. That's when you can turn to design professionals. Several kinds of landscape-design professionals can help.

■ Landscape architects plan and design complete landscapes. The most costly of the pros, they produce drawings, plans, and written work descriptions. They often supervise construction, too.

■ A landscape designer may have less formal training than a landscape architect, but can help you make design decisions and will draw project plans.

■ A landscape contractor builds outdoor structures from plans developed by a landscape architect or designer. A contractor can often suggest solutions to fencing questions.

How do you find them? Start by asking friends and neighbors for references of designers they may have worked with. Your garden shop may have a list of local designers, too.

RAIL FENCES

Rail fences are the first American fences, and their longevity testifies to both their beauty and usefulness. Originally cut by hand from trees cleared to make fields, early rail-fence styles varied from region to region. With advances in milling technology, their style became more uniform, evolving into modern post-and-rail and post-and-board variations. No matter what their style, their simple and modest character recalls their roots as livestock enclosures and uncomplicated boundary markers. These fences are typically 3 to 4 feet high, with posts set a minimum of 2 feet deep.

DEFINING SPACE: Excellent; they make attractive and interesting boundary markers.

SECURITY: Moderate to little; they can impede access but are easy to climb over.

PRIVACY: Minimal.

TEMPERING THE ENVIRONMENT: Minimal; capped rail fences with closely spaced infill can block drifting snow, but little else.

SUITABLE FINISH: Most are best left to weather naturally; post and rail varieties are attractive when stained or painted.

VIRGINIA ZIGZAG

Virginia zigzag fences, also known as worm fences, traditionally were built from split saplings or larger logs. Stacked in a simple zigzag pattern, the angles make them stable.

You can still buy split rails at fencing outlets, but increasingly you'll find sawn rather than hand-split stock. Sawn rails don't have the same rustic appeal as their hand-hewn counterparts. Rails are moderately priced, but a fence requires a lot of lumber—total material costs can be high for a fence that runs a long distance. Construction is fairly time-consuming.

CONSTRUCTION NOTES: Traditional rails are usually 8 to 11 feet long, split from cedar or locust. Pressure-treated dimensioned lumber or landscape timbers—either 4×4s or 6×6s—are good substitutes. Set the bottom rail on rocks to minimize rot. For extra stability, predrill the rail ends and thread each staggered course over ½-inch pipe or rebar. You can set the pipe or rebar in concrete forms or drive it into the ground. Angle each fence section 30 degrees to 45 degrees from the previous one.

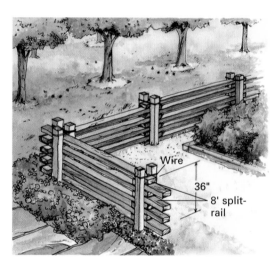

Wire

36"

8' split-rail

KENTUCKY RAIL

Kentucky rail (also called double-post-and-rail) fences represent an early form of post-and-rail construction. These fences can angle across your property, but their design suits them to straight runs—the posts hold the loose rails upright. Rustic and rugged, they require less lumber, which means lower material costs. Construction time is moderate to long.

CONSTRUCTION NOTES: Use split cedar, treated round rails, or landscape timbers (4×6s are easy to handle). Cut rail stock to any length—8 to 12 feet is typical. Set posts of the same or smaller size stock side by side at distances that allow the rails to overlap 12 to 18 inches. Rest the bottom rails on flat stones or fasten them to the posts. Wrap the post tops tightly with galvanized or copper wire, or bridge them with wooden cleats.

MORTISED RUSTIC RAIL

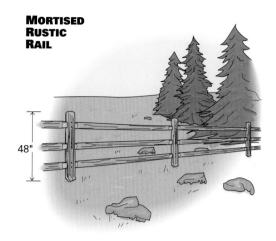

48"

MORTISED POST AND BOARD

48"

NOTCHED POSTS

Fences with rails that fit into notches (called dadoes) in the posts are installed more quickly than mortised fences. But they still present the classic ranch look that adapts to many landscapes. Set the posts before attaching the rails to speed construction. Material costs are moderate.

CONSTRUCTION NOTES: Cut dadoes with a circular saw and chisel. For a 4-foot fence, fasten 1×4 stock to 4×4 posts set 6 to 8 feet apart—set 6×6 posts for a 5-foot fence with 2×6s for rails. Sixteen-foot lumber will span two 8-foot sections—stagger the joints to add strength to the fence. Rails that attach directly to the post faces (with their joints staggered) are easier to build but are structurally weaker and less attractive.

CAPPED POST-AND-BOARD

Capped post-and-board fences are more common in contemporary settings than rail fences. Close rail spacing increases privacy; alternating widths add interest. The cap rail strengthens the structure and enhances the aesthetics of the fence. Material costs are high and construction is time-consuming because this style requires a large quantity of lumber.
CONSTRUCTION NOTES: Space 4×4 posts at 6 to 8 foot intervals and fasten 1×4s and 1×6s (or 1×8s) directly to the post faces. This spacing and alternating of widths provides a pleasing balance, but try other variations. Stagger the rail joints at each course.

DADOED POST AND BOARD

48"

MORTISED POSTS

Mortised rail junctions are a traditional favorite because they require less post-setting time and material. This classic design, generally with two or three rails, fits almost any landscape.

Building suppliers sell rustic rails with wedge-shaped, tapered, or rounded ends (called tenons) that fit into corresponding holes (called mortises) in the posts. They're ready for installation, but you can also cut your own traditional rails or build your fence with boards or dimensioned lumber. Costs are moderate, but construction is time-consuming.
CONSTRUCTION NOTES: The standard length for split, wedge-shaped cedar, pine, or redwood rails with 4- or 6-inch faces is 6 to 11 feet. Cut your own tenons from rounded rails with a drawknife or saber saw and use the techniques shown on page 63 to cut mortises. For a post-and-board fence, mortise 1× stock in 4× posts. Thicker dimensioned lumber rails need thicker posts—use 6×6s.

Build mortised fences one section at a time—the rails will not fit in preset posts. You can also achieve a mortised effect by centering the rails on the posts in metal hangers, avoiding the need to build the fence one bay at a time.

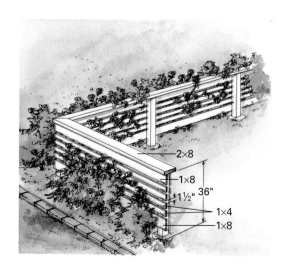

2×8
1×8
1½" 36"
1×4
1×8

BOARD FENCES

Board fences are the most common style of all. They go up easily and adapt to almost all design variations. They're frequently built for privacy and security: They serve these purposes better than most other styles. Over long distances and with uninterrupted surfaces, however, they can seem confining.

Most styles with surface-mounted infill—as opposed to inset infill (see pages 56 and 57)—have one good side where the framing doesn't show. The good side usually faces out, so the neighbors don't have to look at the framing. Inset infill makes a fence look the same from both sides. Board fences usually reach 6 feet—higher, if necessary, and where codes permit.

Lumber suppliers carry all the materials you need, but don't expect to get by cheaply—board fences use a lot of lumber. Construction time varies with style, ranging from moderate to high.

DEFINING SPACES: Very good, with closely spaced infill; can seem imposing unless the surfaces incorporate distinctive features.
SECURITY: Excellent, especially with closely spaced infill and heights of more than 6 feet.
PRIVACY: Closed styles can provide considerable privacy.
TEMPERING THE ENVIRONMENT: Blocks sun but can force wind into downdrafts.
FINISH: Stain, paint, or allow to weather naturally.

SOLID BOARD

Solid-board fences, constructed with no gaps between infill boards, create a wall-like, imposing presence. A solid-board fence seems to warn "Do Not Disturb." (Tall slat fences will also deliver this message.) They create a fully enclosed, very private space that can feel confining. If you don't need privacy along the entire length of the fence, alternate or lower the height of some of the sections to add variety and open up the view. Solid board fences are good candidates for an open top with lattice panels (see page 30).

Construction is simple, requiring only modest carpentry skills to make the basic wood joints. Materials are readily available, and the cost and time requirements are moderate.
CONSTRUCTION NOTES: Surface-mount 1×6s or 1×8s onto rails, which are set either on edge or flat (see pages 54 and 55) between 4×4 posts spaced from 6 to 8 feet apart.

BOARDS AND SLATS

Leaving gaps between the boards and slats on this fence gives it a sense of refinement and a pleasing rhythm. The semiclosed surface provides an ever-changing play of light and shadow.

Experiment with the width of the infill and the spaces—design is often the result of creative choice. The fence shown below has 1×2s and 1×6s. Try 2×2s—they will cast interesting shadow lines. Alternate the infill height in a regular or random pattern (but make sure you draw the pattern first).

A board-and-slat fence requires a little less material (and budget) than does a solid-board fence. It returns high aesthetic value in the form of simplicity and appealing proportions.
CONSTRUCTION NOTES: Surface-mount infill onto edge- or flat-mounted rails attached to 4×4 posts. Set the posts 6 to 8 feet apart.

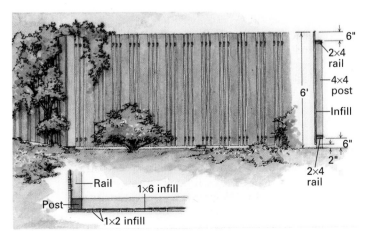

A FENCE IS A STRUCTURAL SYSTEM

Footings, framework, and infill make up a typical fence section, or bay. A solid-board fence is shown, but the structural components of all fences are the same.

FOOTING

The footing keeps the post upright, stable, and rooted in the earth. Every footing consists of three parts:

■ **Posthole** The hole should have smooth, straight sides and be wider at the bottom.

■ **Drainbed** Gravel supports the post base and allows groundwater to drain away.

■ **Filler** Concrete is most often used to anchor the post.

FRAMEWORK

This structural skeleton supports the fence. The components are:

■ **Posts** The posts anchor the fence and support its weight.

■ **Rails** The rails, usually two, connect the posts and hold the fence covering. Rails can be mounted standing on edge or lying flat.

INFILL

This is the covering that forms the surface of the fence.

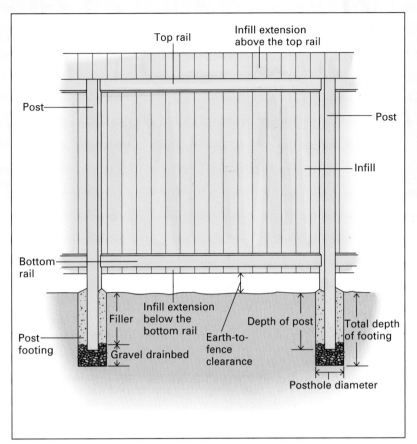

ALTERNATING BAYS

You and your neighbor share both the finished and the framed sides of the fence—in every other bay—with alternating bays. This variation works well with either vertical or horizontal infill (or diagonal infill). You can also alternate the orientation of the boards from horizontal in one bay to vertical in the next. If you don't need privacy along the full length of the fence, your choice of alternating materials might be lattice; flat-rail construction is suited for inset infill, such as lattice or panel frames. Cost and construction time are the same as for a basic board fence.

CONSTRUCTION NOTES: Surface-mount 1×4s or 1×6s (1×8s will look clumsy) to flat rails on 4×4 posts spaced 6 to 8 feet apart (see pages 54 and 55).

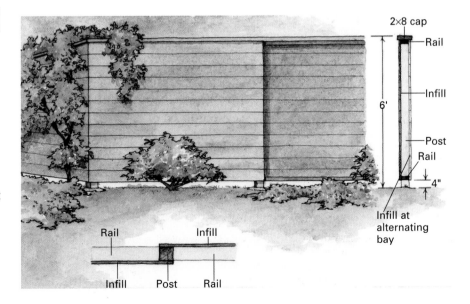

BOARD FENCES
continued

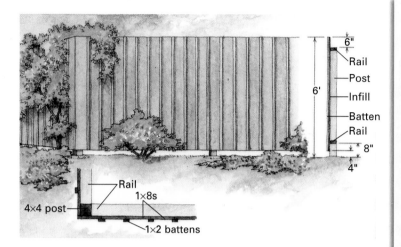

Rail
6"
Post
Infill
6'
Batten
Rail
8"
4"

Rail
1×8s
4×4 post
1×2 battens

DESIGN ALTERNATIVES: MATERIAL SIZES

Materials influence the overall look of your fence. The variety and combination of material sizes and shapes create unique visual rhythms and proportions.

Large structural members look bold and massive. Soften and tailor them with smaller trim details. Small structural members look light and lacy; give these designs extra weight with larger cap rails.

Post spacing—though dictated primarily by structural requirements—affects the rhythm of a fence design. Short spacing moves the viewer's eye rapidly down the fence line. Wide spacing (which may require stronger support) will slow down the rhythm.

BOARD AND BATTEN

In board-and-batten construction, (a form of board-and-slat design), narrow battens cover the joints between wide infill members. The battens create a texture and shadow lines along the infill surface that moderate the tendency of board fences to seem massive. The texture adds style to privacy-fence design. You can lay the infill horizontally, but battens look better in a vertical orientation. Board-and-batten construction is time-consuming and costly, but the aesthetic return is high, making the board and batten a worthwhile investment.

CONSTRUCTION NOTES: Mount the board stock (1×6s or 1×8s) first—to edge- or flat-mounted rails (see pages 54 and 55) on 4×4s spaced 6 to 8 feet apart. Then fasten the 1×2 battens to the boards at each joint.

LAP-JOINT GRID

A lap-joint grid fence makes an attractive screen but doesn't block the view. It looks like latticework, but with wider openings. This open style invites the eye to look at the surface of the materials first, then the pattern they make, and finally the background views. In this way, they provide partial privacy—to a degree controlled by the size of the material and its spacing.

This style is also a two-way fence—your neighbors see the same finished surface you do and have the same limited views into your property as you have of theirs.

You can get a lot of screen for a small amount of material, but construction takes time because you'll need to notch both pieces to create a flush lap joint at each of the intersections of the infill.

CONSTRUCTION NOTES: Space posts at 4- to 6-foot intervals and install flat rails with 1×1 stops positioned so the grid will be centered in the frame. Cut 1×3 or 1×4 board stock to length, measure and mark the position of the intersections, and notch the boards to a 3/8-inch depth with a circular saw and chisel. Predrill the stock and fasten the notches with glue and 1/2-inch-long screws. Then install the grid as inset infill.

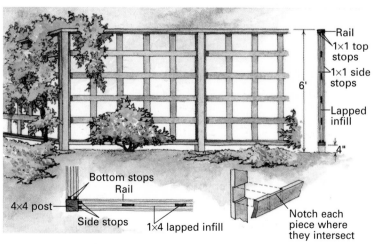

Rail
1×1 top stops
1×1 side stops
6'
Lapped infill
4"

Bottom stops
Rail
4×4 post
Side stops
1×4 lapped infill
Notch each piece where they intersect

BOARD-ON-BOARD

Depending on how much you overlap its infill members, a board-on-board fence can provide full or moderate privacy. No matter what the spacing, this fence will protect you from the wind, breaking it up into little breezes.

In the style illustrated at *right*, the infill is fastened to either side of a central nailer inset on the frame. Inset infill takes some care in fitting and is worth the effort. You get a clean, slim appearance that's attractively scaled on both sides.

Surface-mounted infill—another option—is easier to install. Surface mounting creates more open space between the sides, however, and you will lose some of the gracefulness inherent in this style.

Material costs and construction time for a surface-mounted design are about the same as that of the basic board fence. An inset design requires more time and material.

CONSTRUCTION NOTES: For inset infill, overlap precut 1×6s on a center-mounted 2×2 (or 2×4) nailer fastened to flat rails. (See pages 55 and 57.) Space posts 6 to 8 feet apart and add a middle rail to enhance strength and design variety. For surface-mounted infill, fasten the 1×6s on a flat-rail frame, overlapped by at least an inch.

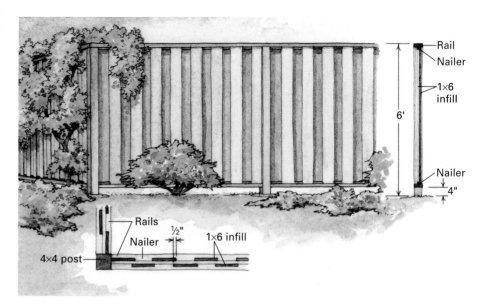

To adapt this fence to small lots, alternate the infill heights—this emphasizes the vertical dimension of the fence and reduces its tendency to look massive.

Materials will cost more and construction time will take longer than for a basic board fence, but the greater investment will reward you with a rich visual effect.

CONSTRUCTION NOTES: Build a flat- or edge-rail frame on posts set from 6 to 8 feet apart. Alternately fasten 1×4s and 1×1s (or 1×2s) to the rails, their edges butted together or separated slightly. If you're varying the infill height, cut the pieces—in a regularly recurring pattern—before fastening them or hang them wild, creating as you go.

ALTERNATING BOARD WIDTHS

Alternating the width of the infill stock is another way of bringing rhythm to a simple, straightforward board fence. Alternating widths also reduce the scale of a board fence, making it seem smaller than it is. The shift from wide to narrow stock sets a pattern that is distinctive, yet calm.

Two other variations offer additional design possibilities. Vary the thickness of the narrow members (use 1×2s, for example) to create shadow lines (a variation of batten design).

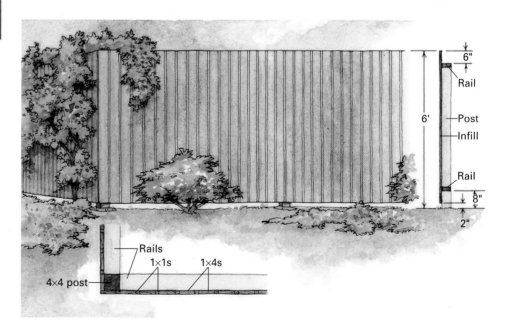

BASKET WEAVE

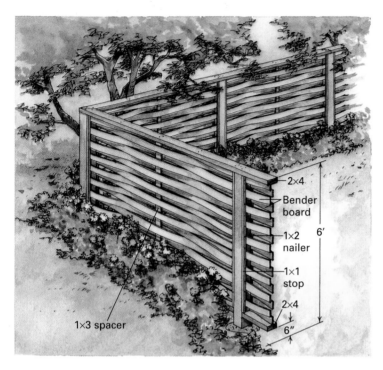

2×4
Bender board
1×2 nailer
1×1 stop
2×4
6'
6"
1×3 spacer

Basket-weave fencing is easy to build, relatively inexpensive, and creates interesting shadow lines. It admits breezes and maintains privacy. Although it is not as likely to feel as dominant as a solid-board fence, it is probably still too much fence for a small enclosure.

Thin boards are woven together around a vertical spacer—one to a bay. These fences look best if the length of the weave is minimized. Very thin materials (available at your local lumberyard) are surprisingly strong and are relatively inexpensive. You'll spend more time building a basket-weave fence than a surface-mounted design, but less than louvered or other fences with inset infill.

DEFINING SPACES: Excellent, but can be too dominant in small areas.

SECURITY: Good; the weave makes a strong—but easy to climb—surface.

PRIVACY: Very good; you can't see through it.

TEMPERING THE ENVIRONMENT: Good for softening winds and blocking sunlight.

FINISH: Paint, stain, or let weather naturally.

CONSTRUCTION NOTES: Build a flat-rail frame on 4×4 posts spaced no further than 8 feet apart. Set the frame up with inset basket-weave nailers and a 1×3 or 2×2 spacer as shown on page 60. Cut, weave, and fasten ⅜- or ½-inch benderboard (redwood is a good choice) in 4- or 5-inch widths to the nailers. Add a 2×4 cap rail.

SUPPORT FOR SAGGING RAILS

All fence designs rely on one of two basic rail positions—rails set on edge or rails set flat. Rails set on edge won't sag as much under the weight of infill because their lateral positioning gives them more strength than rails laid flat. Edge rail designs also offer more choices for ways to mount the infill.

Some designs, however, will work only with flat rails. Most of the styles that require inset infill are examples. Over time—and especially if they have to span more than 6 feet—flat rails will sag. Here are two ways to prevent sagging.

KICKBOARDS: Fasten a 1× or 2× kickboard centered under the bottom rail or under the the outside edge of the infill. Either kickboard acts like an edge-mounted rail and will help keep the bottom rail from sagging.

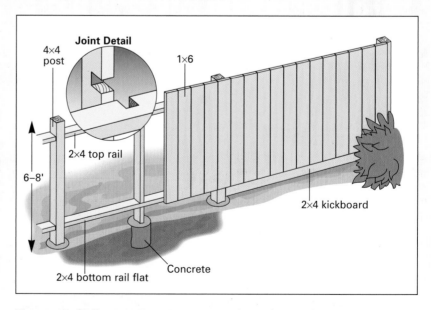

4×4 post
Joint Detail
1×6
2×4 top rail
6–8'
Concrete
2×4 bottom rail flat
2×4 kickboard

NOTCHED 2×4 SUPPORT: Cut a length of 2×4 to fit under the top rail, notch it as shown, and set it in a 24-inch concrete footing.

LOUVERS AND FEATHERBOARD

L ouvered and featherboard fence styles are distinguished by angled infill. The only difference between the two is how closely the infill members are spaced.

Louvers and featherboard fences are best constructed from kiln-dried lumber to minimize warping and sagging, especially on horizontal louvers. Because the boards are angled, it takes more of them to span a fence bay, so louver and featherboard construction requires more lumber and installation time than other board fences. Precutting spacers will reduce construction time somewhat.

DEFINING SPACES: Excellent.
SECURITY: Very good; sturdy and hard to climb from either side.
PRIVACY: Moderate (vertical louvers) to excellent (horizontal louvers and featherboard).
TEMPERING THE ENVIRONMENT: Louvers soften and redirect winds, filter and block sunlight; featherboard does not make a good windscreen.
FINISH: Paint, stain, or let weather naturally.

LOUVERS

A louvered fence, either vertical or horizontal, has a clean-lined architectural look that packs a lot of textural interest. It increases privacy without restricting summer breezes, will filter sunshine for a garden spot planted in its shadow, and makes an excellent pool or patio fence.

Louvers create a surface with patterns of light and shadow; they produce partial privacy by restricting the outside view to only a portion of the yard at a time. Horizontal louvers let you see out but completely block the view from beyond your yard.

CONSTRUCTION NOTES: For a vertical louvered fence, construct a flat-rail frame on 4×4 posts spaced from 4 to 8 feet apart. Cut spacers from scrap 1×3s or 1×4s at a 45-degree angle on both edges. Toenail 1×6 infill to the top and bottom rails, separating them with spacers. (See page 60 for more information on constructing and overlapping louvers.) Finish the fence with a 1×6 cap rail.

For a horizontal louvered fence, build the same flat-rail frame and fasten 1×6 louvers and the spacers to the posts. Build your fence in 4-to 5-foot bays so there is less chance of the horizontal louvers sagging.

FEATHERBOARD

Featherboard fences are classic, condensed versions of the louver style. The closed surface maintains maximum privacy with pleasant shadows and highlights where each board overlaps the next. Privacy is complete, but wind will vault a featherboard fence, descending with equal force on the other side. Material cost is higher than other styles and construction time longer—you must carefully position the overlapped board edges.

CONSTRUCTION NOTES: Build a flat-rail frame and mount a set of 1×1 stops flush with one edge. Toenail the infill (1×4s or 1×6s) to the rails, and when all the infill is mounted, fasten 1×1 stops to the other side. (See page 57 for more information.)

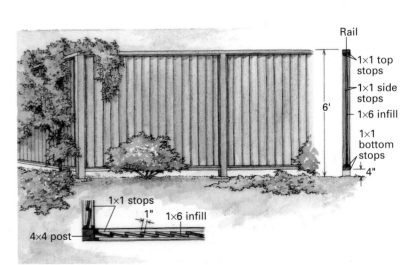

LATTICE

Lattice, a design classic with all its crisscross flair, has decorated gardens and ornamented fences for centuries. Its lines become lively when covered with foliage and its open surface lets in light and evens out the winds.

1×8
2×4
1×1 stops
1×2 lattice infill
6'
3"
8"

Lattice creates varying rhythms and solves various problems with spacing options. Screen out objectionable views with a tight privacy weave. Frame an accent or backdrop tall plants with wider weaves.

Prefabricated 4×8 wood or vinyl panels (in diagonal or rectangular grids) are available at building-supply outlets and lumberyards. And with a little time and patience, you can make your own lattice. Wood lattice comes in two thicknesses—¼ and ¾ inch. The thicker pieces resist warping and cracking, reducing future maintenance—a good return on its slightly higher cost. Lattice is quickly installed and looks best inset in the frame.

DEFINING SPACES: Good; a delightful way to define space or screen an area.
SECURITY: Minimal; easily broken.
PRIVACY: Good; the fence pattern, not the view behind it, holds the eye.
TEMPERING THE ENVIRONMENT: Softens wind and filters sunlight.
FINISH: Paint, stain, or let weather naturally.
CONSTRUCTION NOTES: Build a flat-rail frame for inset infill on posts 4 to 6 feet apart. Install stops, lattice frames, and a 1×8 cap rail. Or, set the panels into channels cut into the frame.

DESIGN ALTERNATIVES: RAIL JOINTS

In each of the fence styles illustrated in this book, the rails are attached in simple butt joints, either between the posts or—for a flat top rail—on top of the posts. Butt joints are the easiest to install and meet the structural requirements for all the designs shown. Fence joinery, however, offers numerous design possibilities. Here are some of them:

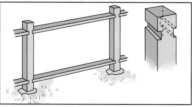

Dado joints are stronger than butt joints and make your fencework look professionally finished. Use dadoes to mount edge or flat rails.

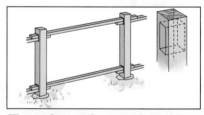

Through mortises can be a thing of beauty, but they must be cut precisely. Use them wherever you want to dress up a joint.

Mitered joints finish overlying cap rails in style. Glue and caulk (after the glue dries) to keep them from separating.

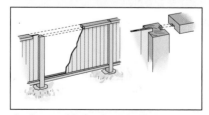

A *channel joint* is a dado cut along the length of rails and posts where panel fencing is inserted. Use it with or without trim.

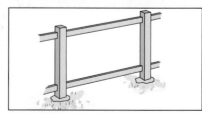

Butt joints are easy to make and are reasonably strong but they can't withstand movement and stress as well as dadoed or mortised joints.

PICKETS

The irrepressible charm and character of picket fences has carried them from cottage to village and from town to city over many generations. They make gentle boundaries, and their classic lines fit well in many types of settings.

Precut ornate pickets and special finials—once readily available—have all but disappeared. Some suppliers still carry precut pickets and screw-on finials in limited shapes, but the retail trend is toward preassembled 3½×8-foot panels—long on convenience but short on originality.

Cabinet shops will mill special orders and a lumberyard might cut pickets for you for a fee. You can cut your own designs, too. Create your own design or pick one of those shown in the illustration *below*. Material cost for pickets is low, but it takes time to properly install a picket fence.

DEFINING SPACES: Good; clearly defines any boundary.

SECURITY: Keeps children and pets in or out, and pointed pickets can make it difficult to hop over.

PRIVACY: Very little.

TEMPERING THE ENVIRONMENT: Will block drifting snow.

FINISH: Paint (especially white) usually looks best, but stain can be effective.

CONSTRUCTION NOTES: Fasten evenly spaced pickets to edge rails on 4×4 posts spaced 6 to 8 feet on center. Use 6×6 posts for fences that are taller than 5 feet. (See page 61 for more information.)

PICKET VARIATIONS

You can pick standard post and picket styles, such as the ones *below*, or design your own for a custom fence. Fancy pickets are fun to design, and they will delight passersby.

First, sketch some ideas, then draw your selected picket top full-size on graph paper. Transfer the design to hardboard and cut out a template. Stack several pickets, trace the hardboard template onto the top one, then gang-cut them. Make straight cuts with a power miter saw so they're all even. Cut curves with hole saws and a saber saw.

PICKET AND POST STYLES

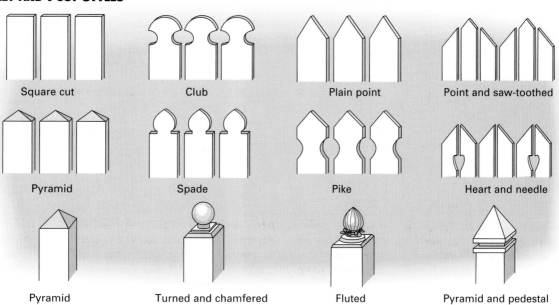

Square cut   Club   Plain point   Point and saw-toothed

Pyramid   Spade   Pike   Heart and needle

Pyramid   Turned and chamfered   Fluted   Pyramid and pedestal

LATH

2×6 cap rail
2×4
Lath strips
36"
2×4
4"

A standard building material once primarily used to reinforce plaster, for shimming, and for lattice work, lath makes an acceptable vertical infill.

Similar to slats and very thin (about ³⁄₈ inch), lath will not withstand rough treatment. (On the other hand, replacing a broken piece is easy.) It should not span rails that are more than 30 to 36 inches apart; attach it firmly at both ends.

Its rough surface will look like a natural part of the garden. Lath is inexpensive and readily available at building supply outlets, but a lath fence has many pieces and will take a long time to assemble.

DEFINING SPACES: Good; similar to slats.
SECURITY: Moderate; fence is stronger with lath nailed to both sides of the rails.
PRIVACY: Lath makes a low (not very private) fence.
TEMPERING THE ENVIRONMENT: Very good for filtering sunlight, softening winds.
FINISH: Unplaned surface is difficult to paint; stain, or allow the fence to weather.
CONSTRUCTION NOTES: Build a flat-rail frame for surface-mounted infill on 4×4 posts set 6 to 8 feet apart (see page 55). Butt the pieces or separate them by ¹⁄₄ inch. Finish the fence with a 2×6 cap rail.

CLEAR ACRYLIC PANELS

A crylic panels make good infill when you want to retain a view or let light in. This material will look out of place in woodland settings, but its clean lines suit modern landscape styles. Its transparency helps if you want moderate security without losing visibility: for example, around a swimming pool or at lake-view property.

Acrylic sheets are sold at plastic and building supply outlets. The cost depends on the thickness of the sheet. Less expensive products fade or yellow with exposure to the sun; these effects won't be as noticeable in tinted materials. Acrylic scratches easily, but polycarbonate (another type of plastic) won't readily show wear. Longer life and lower long-term maintenance may offset its higher initial cost for you. Installation of plastic panels is quick and easy.

DEFINING SPACES: Excellent.
SECURITY: Moderate to good, depending on the strength of the material.
PRIVACY: More like a window than a fence.
TEMPERING THE ENVIRONMENT: Lets sunlight in; tall fences create downdrafts.
FINISH: Paint, stain, apply clear sealer, or let weather naturally (the frame only).
CONSTRUCTION NOTES: Install the panels (¹⁄₄ inch or thicker) as inset infill between stops on flat rails. (See page 64.) Set the posts no more than 4 feet apart to provide rigid support for the panels. If you can't buy them already cut to size, cut the panels with a fine-toothed saw.

2×2 stops
2×4
Acrylic panels
6'
6"

DESIGN ALTERNATIVES: RAIL POSITIONS

Many fence designs in this book feature rails mounted on edge, between the posts, with the infill fastened to the outside face of the fence (the neighbors' side) as shown at right.

With edge rails, you can easily change not only the structure of your fence, but also the way it looks.

For example, you can hang the infill material on the inside fence surface, as shown at the far right.

Also, if you center the rails on the posts, you can inset the infill between the posts.

Or for another modification of edge rail style, you can mount the rails on the exterior faces of the post as shown at right and far right.

This is a popular installation technique largely because it is the easiest. You don't have to cut the rails to fit precisely between the posts. However, you do have to make sure that the rails meet at the middle of a post face.

You can carry the surface-mounting technique one step further by attaching the rails on alternate sides of the posts, as shown at right and far right.

A 1×6 nailed to the end of the fence will hide the otherwise unattractive end-rail joint in surface-mounted rail designs.

RAILS BUTTED BETWEEN POSTS FLUSH WITH OUTSIDE FACE

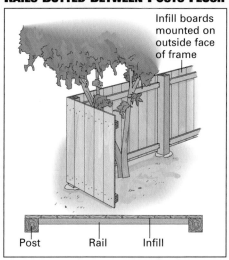

Infill boards mounted on outside face of frame

Post   Rail   Infill

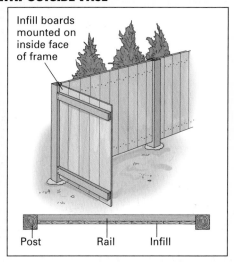

Infill boards mounted on inside face of frame

Post   Rail   Infill

RAILS MOUNTED ON OUTSIDE FACE OF POSTS

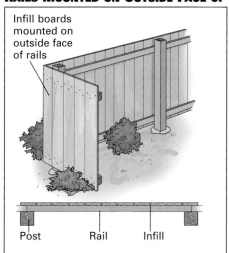

Infill boards mounted on outside face of rails

Post   Rail   Infill

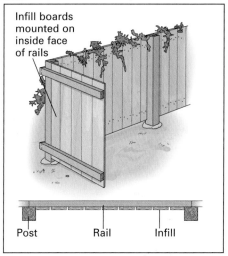

Infill boards mounted on inside face of rails

Post   Rail   Infill

RAILS MOUNTED BAY-BY-BAY ON ALTERNATE FACES OF POSTS

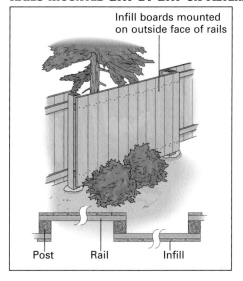

Infill boards mounted on outside face of rails

Post   Rail   Infill

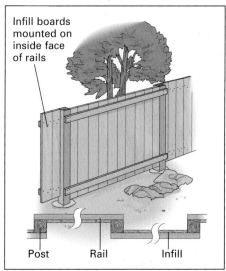

Infill boards mounted on inside face of rails

Post   Rail   Infill

SIDING FENCES

Siding fences allow you to extend the architecture of your house to the landscape. They provide total privacy, and the hollow core of fences finished with shingles and clapboard makes them the best type of fence for blocking noise.

These materials are heavy, so they need to be built on a strong frame. Tongue-and-groove boards and shingles are expensive, and installing them calls for care. You'll save money with finger-jointed tongue-and-groove stock. Protect it with quality primer and paint. Clapboard and plywood are reasonably priced and construction will go quickly. All materials are available at building supply outlets and lumberyards.

DEFINING SPACES: Very attractive dividers; can be overbearing in a small space.
SECURITY: Excellent, especially if the fence is high; impenetrable and difficult to climb.
PRIVACY: Excellent.
TEMPERING THE ENVIRONMENT: Blocks noise, sun, and snow; can cause downdrafts.
FINISH: Clapboard—paint both sides; tongue and groove—paint, stain, or apply clear sealer; plywood—paint or stain; shingle—paint, stain, apply clear sealer, or let it weather.

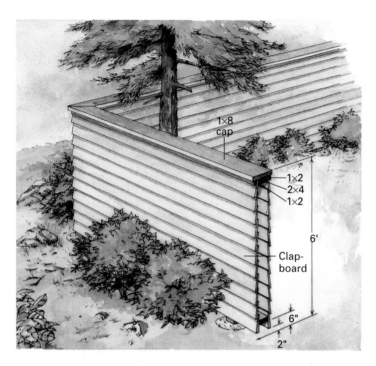

1×8 cap

1×2
2×4
1×2

6'

Clap-board

6"

2"

CLAPBOARD

Extremely attractive when it matches your home siding, clapboard gives a fence an architectural quality, tying it more to the home than to the garden. It still makes an excellent backdrop for many plants, no matter how your home is sided.

Clapboard fences don't work well on uneven terrain. The center cavity can promote rot, so use pressure-treated lumber for framing.

CONSTRUCTION NOTES: Construct a flat-rail frame (see pages 55 and 64) on posts at 8-foot intervals. Toenail 2×4 studs between the rails every 24 inches on center. Starting at the bottom, nail the siding to the studs or to sheathing attached to the suds. Finish with a 1×8 cap rail.

SHINGLES

The highly textured surface of wood shingles gives a fence a rich and warm appearance. If your house is shingled, this fence can unify the home and garden.

Shingles are sold by the bundle at lumberyards and vary in cost according to the grade. Relatively inexpensive No. 3 shingles have some knots and are specified for walls. No. 1 shingles are made for roofs and will cost much more.

Fasten shingles to a backing surface, such as plywood or furring strips. They last longer with space behind them to allow air to circulate, drying out trapped moisture.

CONSTRUCTION NOTES: Construct a flat-rail frame with pressure-treated studs set on 16-inch centers. Space posts 8 feet apart and sheathe the frame with exterior plywood or 1×4 furring strips spaced to match the shingle length. Starting at the bottom, nail the shingles to the sheathing, keeping the courses level.

2×8 cap

2×4
1×2
molding
Shingles
Plywood

36"

3"

2×4

PLYWOOD

A solid-panel plywood fence can look stylish despite the simplicity of its construction. Because plywood is ordinarily sold in 4×8 sheets, fence designs that call for 4- and 8-foot modules are easiest to build.

Only exterior-grade plywood will withstand the elements. Thickness ranges from ⅜ to ¾ inch in ⅛-inch increments. The single-paneled fence shown in the illustration at *right*, is made of ⅝- or ¾-inch material. Thinner panels can be used on double-faced fences. Choose plywood thick enough to resist bowing in heavy winds.

Textured plywood siding is a good choice for fences, too. It comes in several patterns and textures. Simplify finishing tasks by using primed or prestained material.

CONSTRUCTION NOTES: To build the fence shown in the illustration, make a 3-tier, flat-rail frame on posts set 8 feet apart. Fasten 1×2 molding (see page 64) or install the infill in grooves routed or sawn in the frame. To build a two-sided fence, construct a standard flat-rail frame with 2×4 studs spaced on 16-inch centers (for ⅜-inch panels) or on 24-inch centers (for ½-inch material).

TONGUE-AND-GROOVE FENCE

Because its edges interlock, tongue-and-groove siding creates an extremely solid fence, with a style that will suit almost any location. Shadow lines at the joints interrupt the surface with a subtle rhythm. The fence has an ordered, elegant appearance overall.

CONSTRUCTION NOTES: Construct flat-rail framing on 4×4 posts set 6 to 8 feet apart. Attach stops for inset infill and toenail the 1×3 or 1×4 siding to the posts with the tongue up. Because there is no internal support from one post to another, a thin bead of polyurethane glue should be run on the tongue of each board before tapping in the next one. This glue expands, so you won't need much; and it's virtually indestructible even in the harshest weather. Install the outer set of stops and add a cap rail if you like.

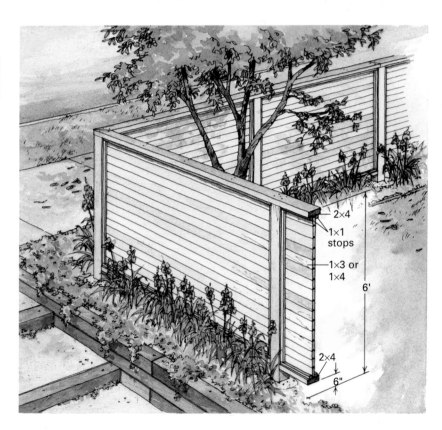

DESIGN ALTERNATIVES: TOPPING OFF YOUR FENCE WITH STYLE

An unadorned board fence can appear massive and imposing, but you can soften that image by opening up the top of the fence. The look of a fence top will contribute as much to its overall style and appearance as the infill you select. Simplicity is the key throughout: Fence-top styles should provide a contrast, not a complication. Here are five ways to dress up your fence:

Rail: This 2×4 cap rail adds a measure of finality to the infill below it. Install a double rail (a 2×6 over a 2×4) for extra strength and variety. Keep the proportions in scale—this design will look best if the posts extend 15 to 18 inches above the main fence height. However, because the top rails lie flat, they will probably sag when spans exceed 4 feet.

Divided rail: In a variation of the rail design, 2×4 blocking supports the 2×4 cap rail every 3 to 4 feet. The blocks add another element of visual rhythm to the fence design and keep the top rails from sagging.

Lattice: If you don't want a completely open top, put in lattice. It affords some screening while it lets the light in and breaks up what otherwise might be an overwhelming stretch of tongue-and-groove infill. After fastening a 2×6 cap rail spanning the posts, install lattice panels in a frame of 1×2s.

Arbor: This arbored top brings a horizontal contrast to the board fence bays. Make the supporting cleats from miter-cut 2×4s or 2×6s. The ends can be cut in decorative curves. Fasten the cleats to the post tops with carriage bolts. Predrill the 2×2 slats before attaching them to the cleats with screws.

Gabled roof: Support a plywood roof with 2×4 rafters and short cross ties. Cut the rafter tails square or decorate them with a design of your choice. Attach the plywood with the best side facing down. You can extend the roof edge past the rafter tails or leave it flush. Cover the roof with composition shingles, cedar shakes or shingles, or other roofing material.

STAKES

Split stakes (or grape stakes) originally made to support plants in vineyards, orchards, and commercial gardens, soon worked their way into a fence design. A handsome, sturdy stake fence has a rich surface texture that easily harmonizes with a variety of design styles, especially rustic or informal ones.

Purchase grape stakes by the piece or by the bundle at lumberyards. Redwood and cedar are rot-resistant and are the most durable. Material cost is moderate but you'll be installing a lot of pieces, so allow plenty of time for construction.

DEFINING SPACES: Excellent, but can be confining in small yards.

SECURITY: Excellent; this is a sturdy, rough-surfaced material.

PRIVACY: Excellent.

TEMPERING THE ENVIRONMENT: Can provide shade but may cause downdrafts.

FINISH: Stain or let it weather naturally.

CONSTRUCTION NOTES: Hang your grape stakes on an edge-rail or flat-rail frame built on posts set 6 to 8 feet apart. Surface-mount the stakes, allowing both top and bottoms to run a bit uneven.

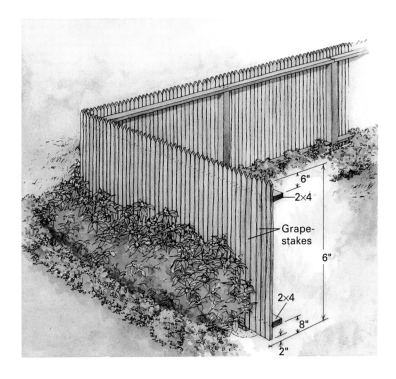

You can also cut the stakes to uniform length and inset them between 1×1 stops.

PALINGS

Saplings split and sharpened to a point are called palings or pales, from an old word for pole. A paling fence, commonly referred to as a stockade fence, works well in wooded settings or woodland landscape designs. It provides excellent security and privacy.

You'll most likely find palings at lumberyards that specialize in fencing materials. If they don't stock them, they may be able to special order them for you. Palings are expensive; and because of its many pieces, a paling fence takes a long time to build.

DEFINING SPACES: Palings create such a strong feeling of enclosure that they are best used as perimeter instead of accent fencing.

SECURITY: Very good; a paling fence is a scaled-down version of a stockade wall.

PRIVACY: Excellent; creates total privacy.

TEMPERING THE ENVIRONMENT: Blocks snow and sun; makes a modestly effective noise barrier because a paling fence is more dense than a board fence.

FINISH: Let weather naturally.

CONSTRUCTION NOTES: For the fence shown at *right*, build a flat-rail frame on 4×4 posts set 6 to 8 feet apart. Palings can also be surface-mounted on an edge-rail frame.

SLATS

The height of the fence and the relative narrowness of the slats project a lightness which gives both the fence and your landscape a visual lift. A slat fence makes an excellent background for a Japanese garden.

Lumberyards sell slats by the the piece or by the bundle. Their cost is moderate, although it takes time to assemble the many infill members of a slat fence. Construction can be tedious.

DEFINING SPACES: Good; defines space graciously.

SECURITY: Excellent, depending on how closely the slats are placed.

PRIVACY: Good; the fence feels open but is hard to see through.

TEMPERING THE ENVIRONMENT: Will block drifting snow and is excellent for softening breezes and filtering light.

FINISH: Paint, stain, or let weather naturally.

CONSTRUCTION NOTES: Build a flat-rail frame on 4×4 posts set 6 to 8 feet apart. Fasten the slats 1 inch apart. (A spacing of roughly ½ the board width will produce a surprising level of privacy.) You can also install slats as surface-mounted infill on an edge-rail frame.

Similar to pickets, but taller and not usually pointed, slats make a fence with simple, crisp lines.

DESIGN ALTERNATIVES: FINISHING OFF THE INFILL AND CAP RAILS

Trimming the top of the infill pieces to different shapes is one way to enhance the appearance of your fence.

A cap rail—a flat-laid rail that runs across the top of the posts and infill—is another fence-top option. Infill and cap-rail finishes (such as the ones shown here) are important and often overlooked elements in establishing a style.

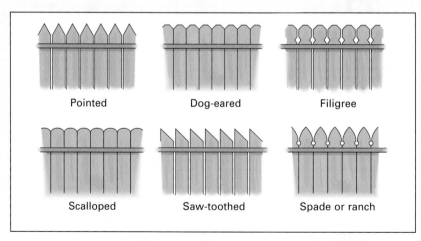

Pointed   Dog-eared   Filigree

Scalloped   Saw-toothed   Spade or ranch

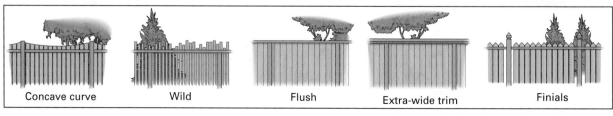

Concave curve   Wild   Flush   Extra-wide trim   Finials

BAMBOO

Bamboo is a grass with amazing properties. It grows fast, and its woody stem is strong and weather-resistant. These qualities, along with its warm, soft color, make it an excellent fence material with a personality all its own.

You can wire-tie bamboo in grids, or weave it and attach it to a frame, as shown in this popular and easily constructed design. Or you can save yourself the work by buying panels that are already wired at home improvement and gardening supply outlets. If they don't stock bamboo, try a mail-order firm. Suppliers can provide you with other design and construction details.

DEFINING SPACES: Good; gives a pleasant, informal feeling of enclosure.

SECURITY: Poor to excellent, depending on the style and size of bamboo used; a bamboo stake fence is very secure; a bamboo grid fence is not.

PRIVACY: Poor to good.

TEMPERING THE ENVIRONMENT: A closely spaced design can soften winds, block snow, and provide shade.

FINISH: Let weather naturally.

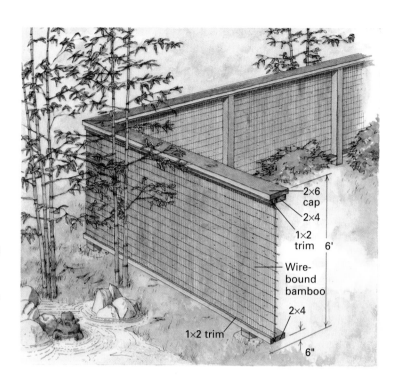

CONSTRUCTION NOTES: Set 4×4 posts on 6- to 8-foot centers and wire panels or 1-inch or larger stems in 4- to 6-inch "windows."

CHAIN LINK

Chain link merits an "excellent" rating as a swimming-pool or children's play-area enclosure because it provides security and doesn't require much maintenance. Special treatments soften the austere look of its zinc or aluminum coating.

Vinyl-clad chain link—in white, green, black, and brown—comes with matching-colored sleeves for posts and rails. Wood-slat inserts, stained to resemble redwood, make chain link an attractive backdrop for vines. Plastic and metal inserts also come in a wide selection of colors. One variety makes the mesh look like a closely cropped hedge.

Almost all home improvement centers and building supply outlets stock chain link in 4-, 5-, and 6-foot heights. With a few rented tools, installation is only moderately difficult.

DEFINING SPACES: Good, but in a very strict, utilitarian manner.

SECURITY: Excellent; chain link was designed for security.

PRIVACY: Very little without inserts; with slats or plantings, moderate to good.

TEMPERING THE ENVIRONMENT: Can block drifting snow but little else.

FINISH: None is required.

CONSTRUCTION NOTES: Set posts no more than 10 feet apart and fasten mesh with hand tools and a rented fence stretcher. (See *page 67*).

WIRE-BOUND FENCES

When you're looking for a temporary solution for a spot that needs fencing—a fence that will go up quickly—wire-bound wood slats or reeds will often do the job. Made of regularly spaced slats or reeds joined by woven wire, both materials come in rolls, and most lumberyards and home improvement centers will carry them. You can also order wire-bound reeds from mail-order outlets. Neither material is expensive, and you can set either up quickly.

DEFINING SPACES: Good, but temporary.

SECURITY: Suggests security, but it is not sturdy.

PRIVACY: Wood slats won't provide much privacy; reeds are better—you can't see through them.

TEMPERING THE ENVIRONMENT: Wood slats are an excellent low-cost way to block drifting snow. Reeds are good for blocking sun and drifting snow; strong winds could tear it.

FINISH: Let weather naturally.

WIRE-BOUND WOOD SLATS

If you need a quick picket border for a newly planted garden and you don't have time to install permanent fencing, wire-bound wood slats are the answer. Often called "snow fence" for its most common use, slat fence will easily get you through a couple of seasons with a minimum investment of time and money. After a few years, however, the weather will take its toll on this fence. In the meantime, a quick coat of dark spray stain and a planting of annual vines will improve its appearance.

CONSTRUCTION NOTES: Build a flat- or edge-rail frame on 4×4 posts set from 6 to 8 feet apart and install the slats as surface-mounted infill. For a temporary snow fence or for quick and easy pickets, wire the slats to metal posts. Roll and wire them to a corner post when not in use.

WIRE-BOUND REEDS

Made from freshwater reeds woven in 4-inch bundles into a weft of lightweight, noncorrosive wire, wire-bound reed fencing can bring a touch of the exotic to your backyard borders. This fence might look out of place in traditional surroundings, however.

Because the reeds are flexible and break easily, durability is not their strong point. But you can get longer service from this fence if you secure the reeds with 1×2 trim fastened to the top and bottom rails. Adding an intermediate third rail centered horizontally between the rails will also strengthen it. Staple the infill to this third rail.

CONSTRUCTION NOTES: Treat the wire-bound reeds as surface-mounted infill; hang it on flat- or edge-mounted rails.

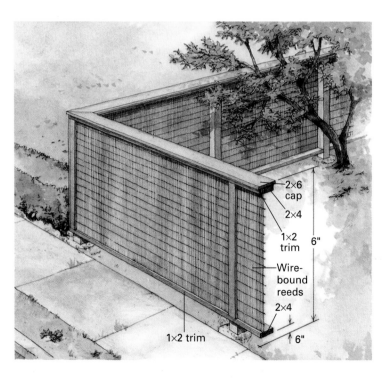

WIRE MESH

Wire mesh is manufactured in many patterns and sizes. Each style has a specific purpose, which is usually to contain animals, from chickens and rabbits to horses and cattle.

The grids create a fence that combines security and protection with good looks. Wire mesh also is good for edging a garden, where it also can provide support for growing plants.

This fence material is inexpensive and you can purchase it in rolls at lumberyards, building supply outlets, and garden centers. It is also available in complete fence, post, and gate packages (in various colors) at a higher cost. With roll fencing, once you set the posts, the rest is easy.

DEFINING SPACES: Defines space in a simple and functional way.

SECURITY: Good to excellent, depending on wire gauge and grid size.

PRIVACY: Very little, unless you train climbing plants onto it.

TEMPERING THE ENVIRONMENT: Not suited for altering environmental conditions.

FINISH: None is required.

CONSTRUCTION NOTES: Staple the mesh

to 4×4 posts on 6- to 8-foot centers. Start at one corner with a full turn of fence around a post, then use a fence stretcher to pull each section tight before stapling it.

WYOMING SNOW FENCE

Researchers have found that Wyoming snow fences work better than other types. Its horizontal 1×6 rails spaced 6 inches apart create an ideal 50 percent porosity. A 10-inch gap at the bottom prevents extensive drifting at the fence line, which can quickly bury a fence and render it useless.

No matter what you use, don't put snow fence right next to a driveway or sidewalk. Keep it at least 30 times its height from the protected area.

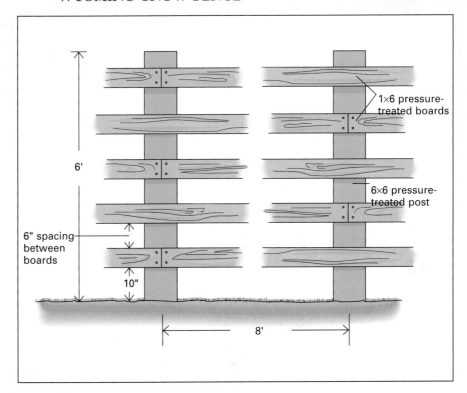

ORNAMENTAL METAL

Welded tubular steel

6'

Most iron fences require bay-by-bay installation and do not leave much room for error. Iron fences require maintenance—frequent painting and wire-brushing—to keep them attractive and rust-free.

Tubular metal fences offer an attractive alternative to forged iron. From a distance, they appear to be forged iron. In the right setting, they look sophisticated and ornate. You can adapt them to landscape installations that range from formal to free-form.

Tubular steel and aluminum fences are also much easier to install than wrought-iron fences. Most come with durable factory finishes, too. Some installation packages include prefabricated fencing sections, posts, flanges, and the fittings to put them all together. These prefabricated products are available at home improvement centers and building supply outlets.

DEFINING SPACES: With narrow spacing, good for surrounding a pool or clearly marking a border.

SECURITY: Very good if the fence is high enough and the infill pattern is small enough.

PRIVACY: Very little.

TEMPERING THE ENVIRONMENT: With narrow spacing, may block drifting snow.

FINISH: Some materials require paint.

CONSTRUCTION NOTES: Tubular metal fences are usually sold as kits, complete with posts, panels, and hardware. Metal posts require concrete footings. When planning a metal fence, get specifications from the manufacturer or distributor.

Ornamental metal fencing—often called wrought-iron fencing—was once forged from iron. Today, tubular steel and aluminum are replacing iron.

Nevertheless, you can probably find a blacksmith or ironworks that still makes wrought-iron fences and gates in traditional styles or custom designs. Expect to pay a lot for the fence and to work hard to install it.

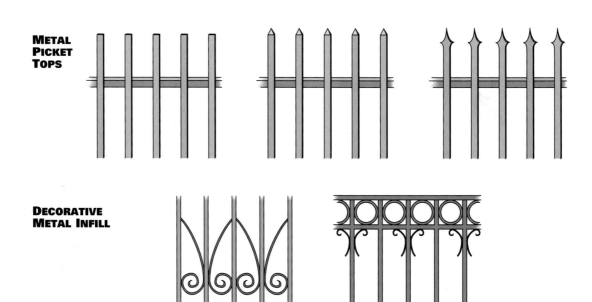

METAL PICKET TOPS

DECORATIVE METAL INFILL

GARDEN FENCES

A tall, formal fence isn't always the answer to landscape fencing. It's often the little things that count. Garden plots are a case in point.

Whether you've tilled and planted full-size, grade-level gardens, built raised beds or walled-in planters, or just have a collection of plants in pots, gardens often need definition. It's something that separates them from other areas and activities in your yard. And you'll usually want some way to guide traffic around or through gardens.

Something that separates the garden from the rest of the yard is just a gentle reminder not to walk on the plants—you don't need a 6-foot fence for that.

In other cases—at the edge of a formal garden path, for example—the garden boundary marker should be welcoming. Chain link won't do.

Low garden fences meet these requirements. They are built where they have nothing to hide; indeed, their job is to help put the garden on display. These fences must complement the garden, blending in and keeping a low profile that helps maintain harmony among all the garden's elements.

Shown here are just three of the many styles you can build quickly and inexpensively. Whatever style you choose— whether one of these or your own design— keep your garden fences low: 18 to 24 inches will do nicely.

The 2×6 on 4×4 posts (*upper right*) is perhaps the easiest to build and the least costly. Set the posts 24 to 30 inches apart and nail or screw the 2×6 centered on them. This little fence offers a place to sit and can save you the stooping and bending that are always a necessary part of garden care.

Grape stakes on 2×4s (*center*) go well in woodland, rustic, or informal gardens. Set the posts 2 feet deep in tamped earth (concrete is good, but not necessary). Leave enough 2×4 exposed to allow 6- to 8-inch spacing between the rails.

Stacked landscape timbers (*bottom right*) don't require posts at all. They make a substantial barricade that looks wonderful in extended lengths—even better when angled around a contour. This fence is all rails; keep them together with lengths of ½-inch pipe or rebar driven through holes drilled through the timber ends and at least 24 inches into the soil. Landscape timbers or redwood posts cut to 24- to 36-inch lengths work well for this type of fence.

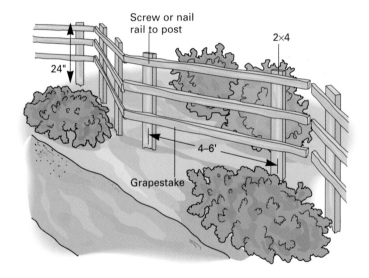

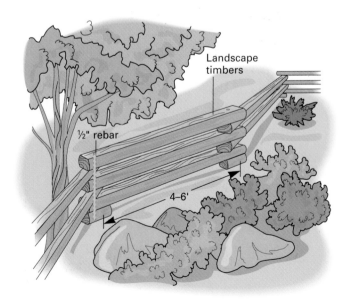

30-60-90 triangle

Architect's scale

Compass

T square

Circle template

Planning Tools: *A few drafting tools will help make your plan drawings uniform.*

Buy an architect's scale—a ruler that translates dimensions into scale sizes. For example, in a drawing in which ¼ inch equals 1 foot, 7 feet would equal 1¾ inches. With an architect's scale, you don't have to figure that out, just draw a line that measures 7 feet on the scale.

You'll also need a compass and a circle template with circles from ½ to 3 inches in diameter. Even if your landscape doesn't have circular structures, these tools help you symbolize round forms, such as trees.

Buy graph paper with ¼-inch squares and drafting tape to stick it to the drawing board or table. A T square will help keep the lines straight and parallel.

PLANNING FENCES

Now it's time to draw your fencing plan on paper. You've looked around your property and mapped the predominant features of your landscape, so you have a pretty good idea about the problems you want fencing to solve. You've decided on fence styles you like and general locations for them.

A fencing plan formalizes all of this. It begins with a base plan, which shows all the features of your yard drawn to scale. Next, you'll develop a site analysis by tracing over the base plan and recording the notes you've kept about your yard. These might include sun and wind patterns, traffic flow, any changes or enhancements you want to make to activity areas, and comments about how fencing can help make those changes.

The site analysis will lead you to a final fencing plan, complete with dimensions and notes about locations. Finally, for each fence, you'll draw a bay sketch—a rendering that illustrates the details of fence construction. Bay sketches help when it comes to making materials lists and estimating costs. A bay sketch also serves as a working drawing— the instruction sheet—for building the fence.

This low, open fence marks the entry walk in style and it harmonizes with the architecture of the home. Planning ensures that the fence meets the needs you identified.

BASE PLAN AND SITE ANALYSIS

Pencil and paper planning is the best insurance for making sure your final fence design meets your expectations. A base plan will get you started.

A base plan is a scale drawing of all the permanent features of your property, including major plantings and structures. It includes lot lines, distances from one object to another, and the dimensions of areas in which you plan to build a fence.

Use the plat map of your property as a foundation for the base plan. You may find one in the closing documents of your house sale, but you can also get a copy from the local government office that records property deed transfers.

Take the plat map to a copy center and enlarge it to a scale that fits the scale you've chosen (for example, ¼-inch equals 1 foot). Then, sketch features that have been added to your yard after the map was drawn.

DRAWING A BASE PLAN

Using your plat map as a guide (or the property sketch you've made), take field measurements. Have a helper hold one end of a 50- or 100-foot steel tape and measure the perimeter of your site, the size of the permanent features in your landscape, and the distances between them—include the house, driveway, patios, walkways, and garden beds. Record the dimensions.

Transfer your field measurements to the plat map enlargement. Plot out the property lines and the dimensions of the site features you measured. Work lightly in pencil. When everything is in place and the site is visually represented, go back and darken the lines. Note the distances between landscape elements on your map. Don't worry if your drawing doesn't look like an architect drew it; if it is accurate and legible, it will work.

BASE PLAN

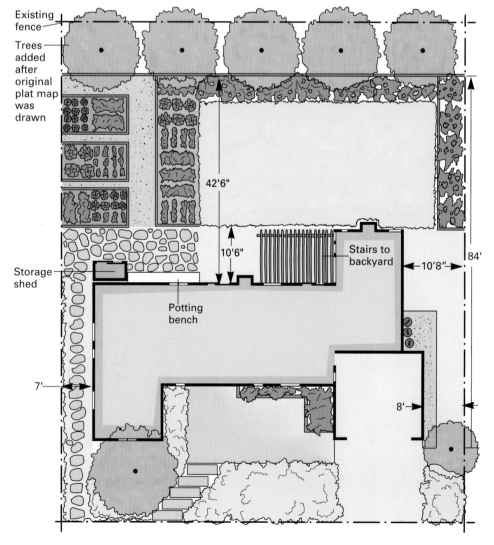

ANALYZE YOUR SITE

Now it's time to add your proposed fence lines. Before you rough in the outlines on paper, be sure of the job each one has to do.

Take a look at your landscape from three perspectives—from inside the house, from the outdoors, and from the neighborhood beyond your property lines. As you do that, consider:

■ What features you like and want to retain. What elements you want to accentuate. What you want to camouflage or hide in the yard.

■ Where the activity areas are, what they are used for and when they are used.

■ Where the traffic patterns are. You may have many—from the street to the house, from the house to the outside areas, and between areas.

■ How wide openings in the fence should be to accommodate traffic.

■ What surrounding views you would like to retain and which views you want to block.
■ Sight lines into your property you would like to block.
■ Places in the yard you would like to shield from a particular vantage point.
■ The prevailing wind direction. Identify areas where you want to temper the wind or wind-blown snow and rain.
■ Sources of noise would you like to block or absorb.
■ Where the sun rises and sets in relation to your property.

A good way to record your findings and see a bird's-eye view of how all these factors work (or might not work) in your landscape is to represent all of them on a single drawing called a site analysis. Here's how to make one.

Tape a piece of tracing paper over your base plan and make notes that reflect the findings from your survey and any other concerns you've recorded. Draw circles to represent distinct activity areas, arrows for traffic paths (including those the children make on their own), wavy lines for winds (see illustration, *below*). Finally, sketch your new fence lines lightly with a pencil. You may want to experiment with different locations now that you have an overall view of the workings of your yard.

This analysis of your property helps you see how each of the various elements can affect the placement of your fences. After studying the site analysis, you can plot fence lines with full confidence they will accomplish your goals.

Even if you decide that your budget or your time won't let you make all of the fencing improvements at once, your site analysis will help you plan future projects to tie in with the fences you build now.

SITE ANALYSIS

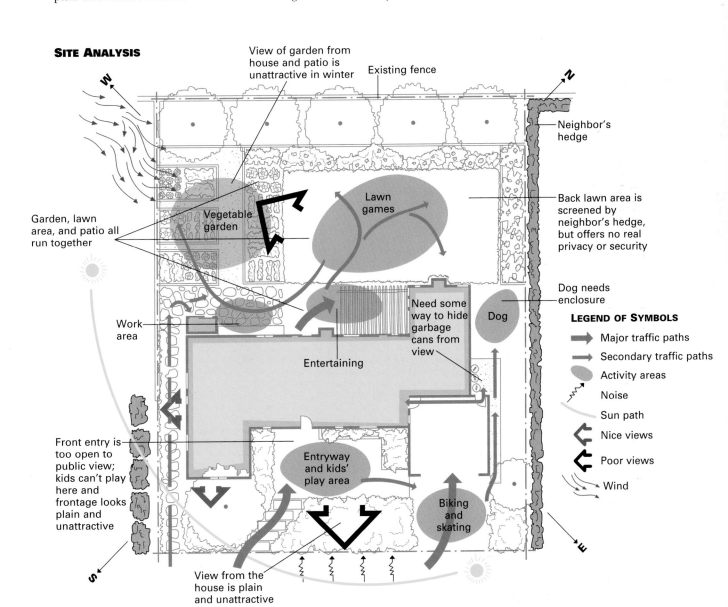

View of garden from house and patio is unattractive in winter

Existing fence

Neighbor's hedge

Back lawn area is screened by neighbor's hedge, but offers no real privacy or security

Garden, lawn area, and patio all run together

Lawn games

Vegetable garden

Dog needs enclosure

Work area

Need some way to hide garbage cans from view

Dog

Entertaining

LEGEND OF SYMBOLS
→ Major traffic paths
→ Secondary traffic paths
⬭ Activity areas
⋏ Noise
⌒ Sun path
◄ Nice views
◄ Poor views
≋ Wind

Front entry is too open to public view; kids can't play here and frontage looks plain and unattractive

Entryway and kids' play area

Biking and skating

View from the house is plain and unattractive

DRAWING A FINAL PLAN

Your site analysis will give you a clear picture of all the the factors that affect the comfort and enjoyment of your landscape. With a little study, it will suggest alternate solutions.

For example, in this site analysis drawing (see page 41), the yard and garden need to be separated from each other. A high fence along the walkway would separate the garden from the yard, but might also seem confining. A 4-foot fence would solve the problem and still block the view of the unplanted garden in the winter. Similarly, in the front yard, where privacy and play need to be balanced, a property-line fence would improve privacy but would not define the children's play area.

Moving the fence back to the front of the patio satisfies both needs effectively.

This is the time to experiment. Don't spend a lot of time on any one layout scheme—you'll have more fun and find the best solution if you work freely and quickly.

THE FINAL PLAN

When your ideas are clear, trace a new drawing of your property. Lay in the final fence lines. Leave a break in the line to show where gate openings will be. Record the overall dimensions of each fence. Note the direction of the gate swing. Now you're ready to plot the length of the bays.

FINAL PLAN

Compare the issues identified in the site analysis on *page 41* with the final plan; note how specific fencing has been used to solve landscaping problems

A 4-foot grapestake fence screens the vegetable garden from view

With perimeter and garden fencing, each area has more definition and proportion

Stepped basket-weave perimeter fence for privacy and security

High scalloped pickets add privacy to front area, provide backdrop for low shrubs, and protect the play area

Chain link confines the dog; the area is large enough for his comfort

The new fence prompted minor landscaping changes to enhance the overall look of the house and yard

Vine-covered lattice frames conceal the refuse area

■ Terminal posts

□ Intermediate posts

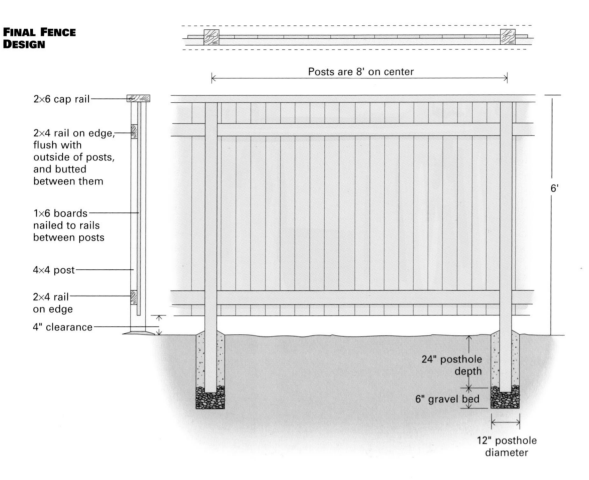

FINAL FENCE DESIGN

Posts are 8' on center

2×6 cap rail

2×4 rail on edge, flush with outside of posts, and butted between them

1×6 boards nailed to rails between posts

4×4 post

2×4 rail on edge

4" clearance

6'

24" posthole depth

6" gravel bed

12" posthole diameter

DIVIDING THE FENCE LINE

Pick any fence line on your final plan and divide its length by the on-center post spacing you want. You'll probably wind up with a remainder, but there are three ways to deal with it:

■ Shorten or lengthen the fence lines to get rid of the odd-size bay.

■ Split the remainder in half and assign it to the two end bays. They will be symmetrical, even though a different size than the rest.

■ Change your post spacing so that each bay absorbs the remainder equally.

When you've decided on the bay lengths, note them on your plan to indicate the length of each bay and how many posts you need.

MAKING A BAY SKETCH

Sketching one bay in detail provides you and your supplier with the exact dimensions of each fence section. To make the sketch, tape a piece of tracing paper over a sheet of graph paper. Then, sketch in a baseline to represent the ground. Plot the framework (posts, rails, and footings) in a scale of 1 inch to 1 foot.

Then tape another sheet of tracing paper over the first one and sketch in the infill and any special details. This way, if you

need to erase any infill, the framework remains intact.

When all the parts are in place, trace the framework from the bottom sheet onto the top one so that the whole drawing is on the same page. Then, write in the dimensions of each component of the fence and the overall height and width of the bay so that every aspect of the plan is recorded.

OTHER DRAWINGS

A bay sketch is probably the only drawing you'll need to order materials and plan construction, but a scale drawing of the complete fence is sometimes useful. If obstacles such as rocks or buried pipes might interfere with digging postholes, a plan view of the fence will help you to plot post locations to avoid them. A scale drawing of at least three or four bays will also help you verify whether you can cut long fence members (such as continuous top rails) from the lengths of lumber you are ordering.

For example, if your posts are 6 feet on center, 12-foot rail stock will span two bays, but will not be long enough to completely cover the end posts. You will need at least two 14-foot rails. Detailed drawings will help you discover such discrepancies.

SLOPES AND OBSTRUCTIONS

STEPPED FRAMEWORK

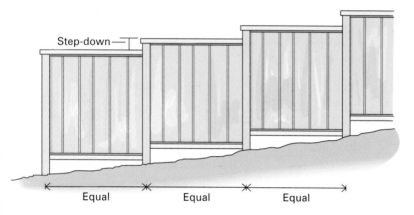

Step-down

Equal　　　Equal　　　Equal

CONTOURED FRAMEWORK

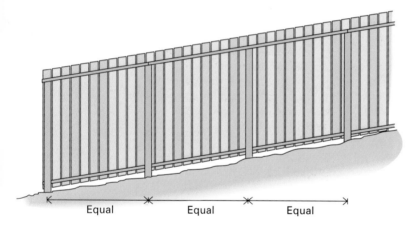

Equal　　　Equal　　　Equal

STEPPED AND CONTOURED

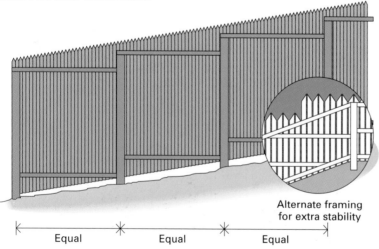

Alternate framing
for extra stability

Equal　　　Equal　　　Equal

Sloped terrain requires special solutions when you're planning your fence design. So do trees, rocks, and other obstacles that fall directly in the fence line. With a little forethought and some careful planning, you can keep these conditions from causing trouble when you begin building your fence.

One of the most common situations you'll probably encounter is fencing on the slope of a hill. Dealing with slopes is a matter of finding the configuration that best fits the grade. The illustrations at left show three solutions. If you aren't sure which framework will work best in your situation, gauging and plotting the slope will help you decide. If you choose a stepped framework, gauging and plotting the slope will help you determine how much each bay must rise above the one below it.

GAUGING A SLOPE

There are several ways to gauge a slope—to determine its rise and run. This simple method is enough for most situations. You'll need a length of mason's line, stakes, and a line level.

■ Drive two stakes firmly into the ground, a short one at the top of the slope and a long one at the bottom (see page 45).

■ Tie the line to the top stake at ground level. Make sure the line doesn't touch anything (cut away the grass, if necessary), hang the level in the middle of the line, and stretch the line to the other stake.

■ Pull the line tight and tie it to the down-slope stake. Adjust the line until it's level, then mark the stake where the line crosses it.

■ To determine the rise, measure from the mark to the ground. To determine the run, measure the line from stake to stake. Write down both numbers.

■ Leave the stakes in place—they mark the locations of the top and bottom posts. If your slope consists of multiple inclines, follow the same steps at every change in grade.

PLOTTING THE SLOPE

Plot the slope on graph paper (a grid of ¼ inch equals 1 foot works well).

■ Draw a baseline on the graph paper.

■ Plot the measurements of the slope, then connect the points to show the profile.

■ Lay tracing paper over the slope profile. Draw a framework on the tracing paper to see how it would work for your fence. Try different dimensions, sketching each on tracing paper until you arrive at both the style you want and a suitable length of the bays.

CHOOSING THE FRAMEWORK

Consider the slope and the kind of fence you plan to install when deciding on framework.
STEPPED FRAMEWORK: In this style, the bays step down the slope in equal lengths. A stepped framework fits best on gradual, even slopes; the overall effect is uniform and orderly.

Board fences, louvers, and basket-weave styles work well mounted on stepped framework. So do plywood and lattice. (Be sure to mount sheet material inset to the frame, not on its surface.)

To figure the step-down for each successive bay, follow these steps:
■ Count the number of bays in the sloped section. (The fence-line layout you traced should give you this information.)
■ Convert the rise into inches and divide that figure by the number of bays. The result tells you how much each bay needs to rise for the fence to step evenly. For example, if the run of the slope measures 32 feet and its rise is 36 inches, four 8-foot bays would span the length of the slope; and, each of the four bays would step down 9 inches (36/4=9).
CONTOURED FRAMEWORK: In this design, the entire length of the frame follows the contour of the slope. Posts are plumb, but the rails run parallel to the grade. This design will work with almost any terrain—steep or gradual, uneven or rolling.

Post-and-rail fences, narrow boards, slats, pickets, stakes, palings, and wire-bound fencing all work well with contoured frames. Infill must be surface-mounted, not inset.

STEPPED AND CONTOURED: This design combines the best properties of both fences. You'll often find it spanning very steep grades, where an easier-to-build stepped bay fence would leave large triangular voids along the bottom and excessive, awkward-looking step-downs at the top. This design solves those problems with infill that extends beyond the frame and follows the grade.

OBSTRUCTIONS IN THE FENCE LINE

If your proposed fence line goes through tree trunks, rock outcroppings, gullies, or swales, the fence will have to make way. The illustration at right

HOW TO GAUGE A SLOPE

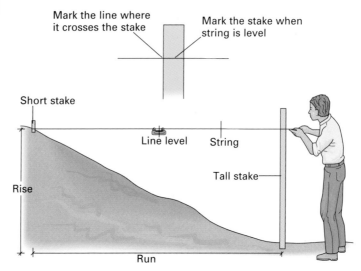

Mark the line where it crosses the stake
Mark the stake when string is level
Short stake
Line level
String
Tall stake
Rise
Run

offers a few uncomplicated compromises you can reach with such obstacles.

It is usually not a good idea to nail fencing to the trunk of a tree. Puncture wounds can expose a living tree to bacterial invasion and generally disturb the flow of water and nutrients. Posts can harm a root system if you set them too close to a tree. Reposition the fence line or stop it short of the tree on either side so the tree can continue to grow. If you have enough room, skirt the tree (or any obstacle) with a curved section of fence (see pages 49 and 59).

FENCING WITH OBSTRUCTIONS

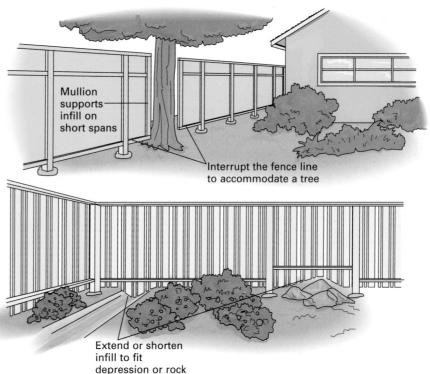

Mullion supports infill on short spans

Interrupt the fence line to accommodate a tree

Extend or shorten infill to fit depression or rock

BUILDING FENCES

You've drawn the plans, had the materials delivered, and gathered your tools. Now it's time to turn your ideas into reality and build your fence. Fence-building includes three phases: groundwork, assembly, and finishing. Most homeowners have the skills to carry out these tasks.

Groundwork consists of staking the layout and digging postholes. Work carefully so the fence runs true. If your plan calls for a lot of postholes, rent a power auger. You can get bit diameters of 8, 10, and 12 inches. But be careful—it takes two strong people to control a power auger.

Assembly includes setting the posts, installing the rails and infill, and trimming. These steps call for basic building skills, but don't worry if you don't have them to start with. You can develop them with your fence-building project. The most exacting and labor-intensive step is setting the posts, because they establish the foundation for the fence. Each post needs to be plumbed, aligned, and braced. Then, you'll have to pour concrete or fill and tamp earth-and-gravel backfill. Installing the rails and infill can be fun, fast, and easy. This is when you start to see your fence take shape.

Finishing means preparing the surfaces and applying sealer, paint, or stain. Applying a finish that looks good and will last takes time. This gives your fence its final appearance, unifying it with the rest of your landscape.

The following pages show the steps for each stage in building your fence.

WORKING WITH PROFESSIONALS

You don't have to do all the work yourself to enjoy the satisfaction of designing and building your fence. You can contract any part of the job you can't—or don't want to—do yourself. But before you get help, look at the costs. In general, you'll spend roughly twice your materials costs for any contracted work.

The best way to find a reputable builder is to ask friends, neighbors, colleagues, or your materials supplier for recommendations. Make a list and interview each contractor. Describe the nature and extent of your project—how many postholes need to be dug, for instance, or how many linear feet of fence need to be assembled or painted. Ask the contractor for references, and check them out.

Next, ask for bids from those contractors that seem promising. Before bidding, a contractor must visit your site to take a closer look at the details of the project. The contractor must see the job to come up with a firm idea of costs, the materials you want to use, and scheduling for the project.

When you accept a bid, ask for a contract that clearly specifies the work that will be done, the time period in which it is to be completed, the quality of materials used, and the cost for each phase of the project. The contract is to protect both parties; you will create that protection by arriving at a shared understanding of the contractor's responsibilities as well as your own.

LAYING OUT THE SITE

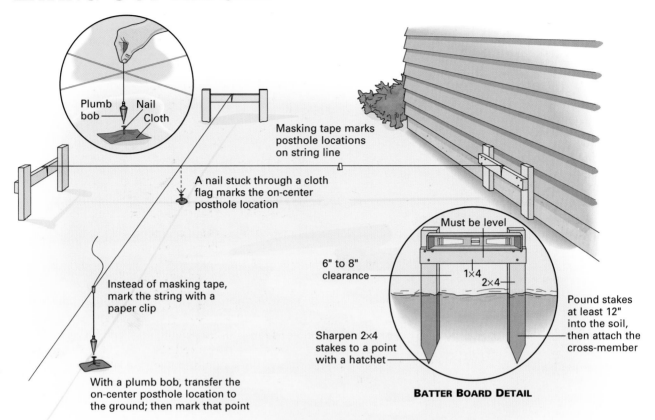

Plumb bob   Nail
Cloth

Masking tape marks posthole locations on string line

A nail stuck through a cloth flag marks the on-center posthole location

Instead of masking tape, mark the string with a paper clip

With a plumb bob, transfer the on-center posthole location to the ground; then mark that point

Must be level

6" to 8" clearance

1×4
2×4

Sharpen 2×4 stakes to a point with a hatchet

Pound stakes at least 12" into the soil, then attach the cross-member

BATTER BOARD DETAIL

Laying out the site is the least strenuous and most critical of the three major fence-building tasks. Proper layout results in fence lines that don't meander. Postholes that are set true will mean trouble-free installation for the rest of the fence.

STAKES AND BATTER BOARDS

The first step is to mark the approximate ends of your fence line with temporary stakes. Then build batter boards—as many as there

are changes of direction or grade in your longest fence line.

Make the batter boards from 2×4s as shown in the illustration above and drive them into the ground about 18 inches past your temporary stakes. If the fence will abut a house wall or existing fence, drive the batter boards just in front of it.

LINING UP

Stretch a mason's line (it won't sag over moderately long distances) between each pair of batter boards. If the distance between batter boards is so long that the line won't stay level, add a batter board midspan and tie a separate line between each pair. Check the line positions. Make each relatively straight and square to the others to start.

Double-check the placement of the lines. Do they correspond to the positions of the fence you drew on your final plan? For instance, if a section of fence runs parallel to the wall of the house, measure from the wall at each end of the line to see if it is properly placed. Adjust as needed.

FENCING ON THE SAFE SIDE

As you stake the layout, remember that no part of your fence—including the concrete footings—should cross property lines. Fence builders often stake out the fence line so that it falls at least 6 inches inside the boundaries, just to be on the safe side.

SQUARING THE SITE

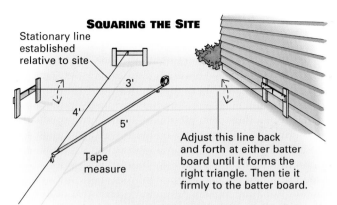

Stationary line established relative to site

3'

4'

5'

Tape measure

Adjust this line back and forth at either batter board until it forms the right triangle. Then tie it firmly to the batter board.

Measure along one line and mark a point at 3' from the intersection. Next, measure along the other line and mark a point at 4'. Then measure the distance between the two marks. Adjust one line until the distance between the marks is exactly 5'. The angle is then a perfect 90°.

During this initial layout stage, your lines represent the center of the fence. Later—when you're setting and aligning the posts—you will reposition the lines to mark the outside face of the posts.

PARALLEL AND SQUARE

Wherever your fence changes direction or terminates against an existing wall, make certain the angle of the intersection is correct. For right angles, use the 3–4–5 triangle technique shown at left. For other angles, a simple sight check with a protractor will probably suffice. For more precision, cut guide angles from cardboard or thin plywood.

WORKING WITH OBSTRUCTIONS

If bushes or other obstructions interfere with the line between the batter boards, your layout won't be precise. If you can remove the obstacle (prop it out of the way or trim it back) do so. If it's a permanent part of the landscape, such as a rock outcropping, use taller batter boards so that the line clears the obstruction.

When you have staked the fence lines accurately as shown on your plan, you're ready to mark the posthole locations.

STAKING OUT A CURVE

Even if you drew the curve precisely on your final plan, you may need to change it to fit the realities of the actual location. You'll need some stakes, mason's line, and a short piece of rebar. Here's what to do:

■ Drive a stake at each end of the arc. Tie a taut line between the stakes.

■ Drive a stake at the line's midpoint and run a perpendicular line toward the inside of the curve (see the drawing at right).

■ Drive a stake along that line as a centerpoint, and tie one end of a line to it. Tie a short piece of rebar to the other end.

■ Swing an arc between the end stakes, scribing a mark on the ground with the rebar. Try different arc depths. Move the pivot stake closer to the line between the arc ends for a deeper arc, away from the line for a shallower one.

■ Scribe a heavy line in the ground for the final arc.

■ Mark the post locations around the arc. You'll need at least three posts to define a curved section. When you set the posts, note their orientation; for most infill styles, the post faces should fall on the arc line.

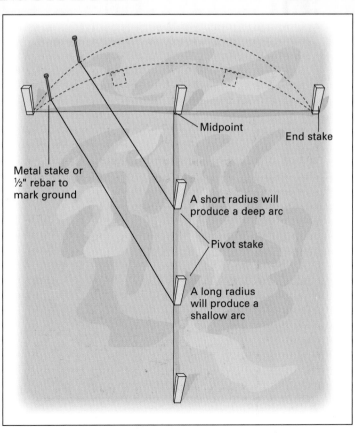

Midpoint

End stake

Metal stake or ½" rebar to mark ground

A short radius will produce a deep arc

Pivot stake

A long radius will produce a shallow arc

LAYING OUT THE SITE
continued

MARKING POSTHOLE LOCATIONS

Before you mark the post locations, measure the fence line again to make sure it's the same length as noted on your final plan. That way, you'll be sure that the post spacings you planned will fill the length of the fence line.

Once you've checked, measure the width of each bay on your layout line and mark the intervals with tape (see page 48). At each piece of tape and at intersecting lines, drop a plumb bob. When it comes to rest, push a roofing nail through a scrap of cloth immediately below its tip. The nail marks the center of your posthole—it's where you'll set your posthole digger.

When you've marked each posthole center, cut a small V-notch in the batter board crossbar where the string line now rests (or mark the spot with an indelible pen). Then untie the lines to provide open access for digging the postholes. Leave the batter boards in place; you'll string new lines between them later to align the posts. The notch will help you find the right position. Then dig your postholes to the depth required for your fence.

POSTHOLES ON SLOPES

Fencing a slope comes down to two options—contoured fencing or stepped fencing. (The stepped and contoured fence shown on page 44 is really a stepped frame with contoured

infill.) The rails of a contoured frame run parallel to the slope and to each other, and the infill is cut to follow the slope. Stepped fencing resembles a stairway—each bay steps down the slope by an equal amount. Stepped-fence rails run horizontally and parallel to each other.

Contoured fencing is easier to install, especially on irregular or rolling slopes. Rail fences and fences with surface-mounted infill make good contoured models. Inset infill does not work well with contoured fencing.

Stepped fences are more difficult to plan and install, so are more suited to straight slopes. Almost any board fence can be adapted to a stepped fence.

Marking posthole locations on a slope requires a different technique than marking them on level ground. If you measure along the ground on a slope, the posts will end up closer together than you want them to be. To space the posts correctly, you must either establish a level line or mark the holes with a layout stick.

To establish a level line, drive a stake at each end of your layout line where the terminal posts will be. Make the lower stake tall enough to be level with the top of the grade (see page 51).

Tie mason's line tightly between the stakes. On short slopes, tie the upper end at grade level and slip a line level on it. On long slopes, tie the line about a foot above grade so you'll have room to use a water level to level the line at the lower stake.

To make a layout stick to locate the posts, cut a 1×2 or 1×4 board to a length equal to the center-to-center distance between posts.

STAKING CONTOURED LAYOUTS

To stake out a slope for contoured fencing, drive batter boards at both the top and bottom of the slope. Make sure they're tall enough to clear obstructions, and tie mason's line tightly

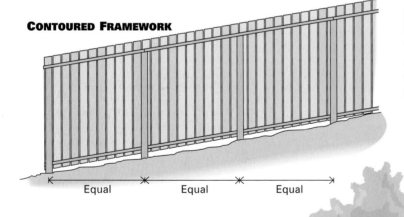

CONTOURED FRAMEWORK

Equal   Equal   Equal

STAKING THE LAYOUT OVER A SLOPE

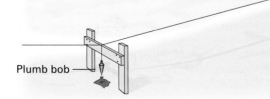

Bay width

Plumb bob

Adjust the line along the batter board until it is directly in line with the level section; wrap it around the cross-member and proceed

between them. If the slope changes abruptly, drive batter boards at every change in grade.

■ First, make sure the line of your fence continues along the same plane as the sections on level ground. Sight along the line from both the bottom of the run and from at least halfway along the line on the level section. Adjust the position of the line on the batter boards until you're satisfied it's correct.

■ If you have established a level line, mark the line with tape at intervals equal to the width of your bays. Then, drop a plumb bob at each piece of tape and mark the center of the post with a nail pushed through a scrap of cloth (see the drawing at right).

■ If you're working with a layout stick, drive a tall stake into the ground, plumb, with its uphill face on the lowest posthole's center. Butt the layout stick against the uphill face of the stake. Holding the layout stick level (lay a level on it), slide it down the stake until the other end intersects the layout line. Mark the line. Move the stake to this position, and repeat the process to mark the next posthole. Continue up the slope. Drop a plumb bob at each mark to find the posthole locations.

■ Dig the postholes.

STAKING A STEPPED FENCE

Stepped fencing requires the same marking techniques used to mark for a contoured fence plus one additional step—measuring the step-down of each bay. (You'll do this after digging the holes and setting the posts in place.)

■ First, establish the fence line and mark the post locations, using either a level line or a layout stick, as described on page 50.

■ Then, measure the exact rise and run and compute the step-down distance using the formula described on page 45.

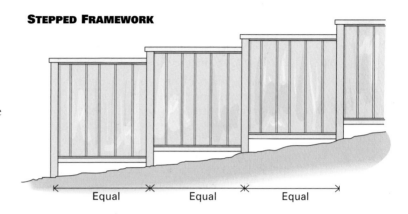

STEPPED FRAMEWORK

Equal   Equal   Equal

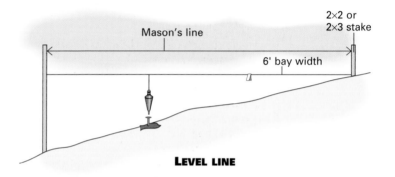

Mason's line

2×2 or 2×3 stake

6' bay width

LEVEL LINE

■ After you've dug the postholes, you can install all the posts. Make sure each stands taller than its final length.

■ When you've set and braced all posts (see page 52), mark the step-down distance—measuring from the top—on the uppermost post. With a water level, mark the next post down the hill at that height. Cut that post to height, mark the step-down on it, and repeat for the next post. Repeat for all of the posts.

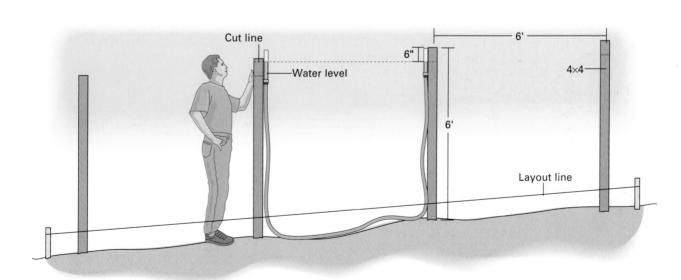

Cut line

Water level

6"

6'

6'

4×4

Layout line

INSTALLING POSTS

Setting posts is the most important part of fence-frame construction. With plumb, perfectly aligned posts, you'll breeze through the rest of the process. Out-of-plumb and poorly aligned posts will mean you'll have to coax wayward parts together with a lot of extra fitting and cutting.

SETTING POSTS

Dadoed or mortised joints require posts cut to a precise height (see page 53). With other styles, let the height run wild and cut the entire line later. Here's what to do:

■ Divide the actual size of your posts by 2 (a 6×6, for example, measures 5½ inches thick) and move your mason's lines this distance away from their original position. This new position will place the line in the plane of the outside post faces, as shown on page 53.

■ Stand an end post in its hole and twist its base into the gravel bed about 2 inches. On two adjacent sides and about two-thirds up the post, pivot 1×4 braces on a single duplex nail (its two heads make removal easy). Then plumb the post on two adjacent faces with a 4-foot carpenter's level or post level, keeping the post face just touching the mason's line. Stake the braces securely, attaching them to the post with a couple of box nails or screws. Repeat the process for the other end posts.

GUIDELINES FOR POSTHOLES

Concrete provides the most stable base for fence posts (especially terminal posts). Earth and gravel backfill, however, may be suitable for low, lightweight fences with posts set in stable soil. In either case, embed the bottom of the post in a 6-inch (about ⅓ cubic foot) gravel bed before setting the footing.

SETTING EARTH-AND-GRAVEL FOOTINGS Starting with a 6-inch gravel bed, alternate earth and gravel in 3- to 4-inch layers. Tamp each layer vigorously with a 2×4 and slope the top.

SETTING CONCRETE FOOTINGS Mix concrete from scratch (about 1 part cement, 1 part sand, and 1½ parts gravel) or use premix. Make it stiff enough to pack into a ball in your hand. Shovel the concrete into the hole and work it with a pipe to remove air pockets. Slope the top to let the rain run off. The mix begins to set up and become rigid in about 20 minutes.

DEPTH AND DIAMETERS Here are some guidelines for posthole dimensions. Consult your local building department for information specific to your area.

POSTHOLE DIAMETER The minimum diameter of the posthole depends on the footing:

■ Earth-and-gravel. Make your posthole diameter at least twice the width of the post. A 4×4 requires an 8-inch diameter, a 6×6, a 12-inch diameter.

■ Concrete footings. Make the posthole diameter at least three times the width of the post. A 4×4 post requires a hole 12 inches in diameter; a 6×6 requires one 18 inches in diameter.

POSTHOLE DEPTH Terminal Posts—As a general rule, ⅓ of the total post length should be below ground (at a minimum depth of 24 inches) and ⅔ above ground. Thus, a 6-foot terminal post should be 9 feet long, set in a 3-foot posthole. Line posts can be set slightly less deep. Line posts for a 6-foot fence can be 8 feet long set in 2-foot holes. Local codes may require depths below the frost line.

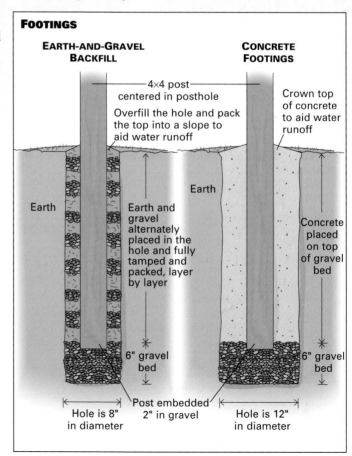

FOOTINGS

EARTH-AND-GRAVEL BACKFILL

CONCRETE FOOTINGS

—4×4 post—
centered in posthole

Overfill the hole and pack the top into a slope to aid water runoff

Crown top of concrete to aid water runoff

Earth

Earth and gravel alternately placed in the hole and fully tamped and packed, layer by layer

Earth

Concrete placed on top of gravel bed

6" gravel bed

6" gravel bed

Post embedded 2" in gravel

Hole is 8" in diameter

Hole is 12" in diameter

■ To help keep the intermediate posts straight, stretch another line between the end posts about 18 inches below their tops. Then set, align, and brace each successive intermediate post.

■ When all the posts are braced, shovel in the footing filler, either earth-and-gravel or concrete (see page 52). Double-check each post for alignment and plumb. If you've installed concrete footings and you plan to fasten the rails and infill with screws, you can cut the posts and build the rest of your fence after the concrete sets. If you're going to nail your fence frame, wait until the concrete cures—three to seven days. In either case, leave the braces in place.

CUTTING POSTS

If you've set the posts with their heights wild, now's the time to cut them to length.

■ Measure one end post from the ground to the post height and mark it. If the grade is level, snap a level chalk line from that point to the other end post. That will mark all posts at the same height. If you're building a contoured fence, measure the same distance up the other end post and snap the chalk line between them. Make sure all posts are marked and resnap the line if necessary.

■ Carry the marks around each post with a try-square. If you're building a contoured fence, you will cut at an angle—carry the marks across the downslope and upslope faces first, then connect these lines on the fourth side.

■ Cut each post to height with a hand saw or a circular saw. You'll be on a ladder, so be careful, and, above all, patient. It may be easier to start the cut around the post with the circular saw and finish the cut with a hand saw. Sharp blades make the job faster and safer.

FIXED-HEIGHT POSTS

Posts with mortises or dadoes need to be set precisely to the same height—a couple of cleats will keep them there. Figure out how much of the post you want above ground, then measure down that distance from the top of one end post. Fasten a pair of cleats at that point (*right*), and set the post in its hole. Plumb, align, and brace it; then repeat for the other end post.

Stretch a line over the tops of the end posts and adjust the cleats until the line is level. Then cleat the remaining posts, using the line to put them at the proper height. Set one end post in its footing, but do not set the rest until you've installed the rails—mortised fences are installed one bay at a time.

ALIGNING AND BRACING POSTS

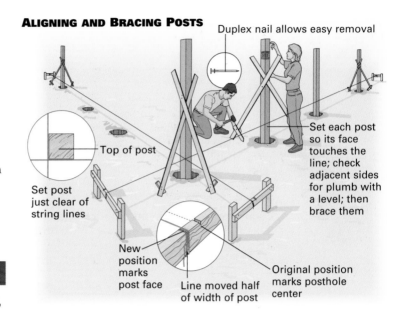

Duplex nail allows easy removal

Top of post

Set post just clear of string lines

Set each post so its face touches the line; check adjacent sides for plumb with a level; then brace them

New position marks post face

Line moved half of width of post

Original position marks posthole center

MARKING POSTS FOR CUTTING

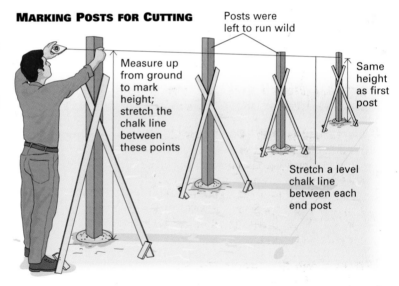

Posts were left to run wild

Measure up from ground to mark height; stretch the chalk line between these points

Same height as first post

Stretch a level chalk line between each end post

FIXED-HEIGHT POSTS

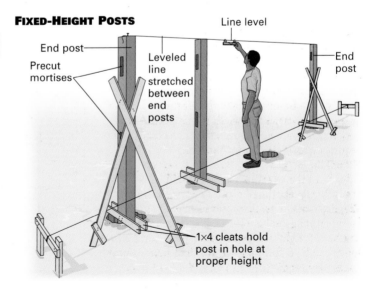

Line level

End post

Precut mortises

Leveled line stretched between end posts

End post

1×4 cleats hold post in hole at proper height

INSTALLING RAILS

Rails for all fence styles are aligned as either edge rails or flat rails.

Edge-rail framing resists the tendency to sag better than flat-rail framing. Both styles will accept surface-mounted infill. If your design calls for inset infill, you will probably need to install the rails flat.

Below are steps for installing rails between the posts. For another option, see *Installing Surface Rails* in the box at right.

INSTALLING SURFACE RAILS

Edge rails mount most easily to the surfaces of the posts. Surface-mounted rails don't require cutting and fitting between posts but do require attention to another detail— their joints. Use rail stock long enough to span at least two (and preferably more posts). Center rail butt joints on the posts. Use the nailing patterns illustrated, and predrill the holes for whatever fasteners you use.

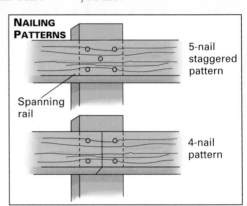

NAILING PATTERNS

Spanning rail

5-nail staggered pattern

4-nail pattern

EDGE-RAIL FRAMING

■ Distribute the rails around the perimeter of the fence line so you can assemble the frame more quickly. Leave the 1×4 braces up, if possible—they add stability when fastening rails and will help keep any slightly bowed posts in line.

■ Mark the top rails for cutting. You can either measure the distance between posts or hold the uncut rail in place and mark it, as shown for the bottom rail in the illustration below. Don't precut all the rails at once because the distance between one or two pairs of posts may be short by a fraction of an inch. This discrepancy won't show when you get the infill up, but rails that are an 1/8-inch short just won't reach. Always saw just to the outside of your mark to make your rail fit snugly.

■ Next, mark both top and bottom rail positions on the posts. (Add a center rail for fences with heavy infill or if the bays span more than 72 inches.) Most of the designs in this book call for upper rails set 6 inches below the top of the post and bottom rails placed from 3 to 8 inches above grade. Whatever the spacing, always measure down from the top of each post.

For stepped frames or for contoured frames over uneven terrain, you'll have to measure and mark each successive pair of posts separately. For frames on level ground or on an even slope, you can mark an entire section of the fence line at once by snapping a chalk line.

■ If your rails will be centered on the post faces, mark the center of both the posts and the cut rails.

BUILDING AN EDGE-RAIL FRAME

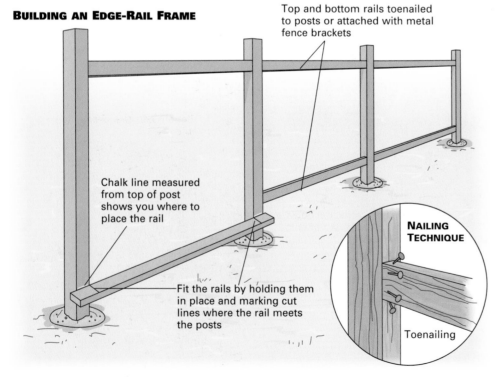

Top and bottom rails toenailed to posts or attached with metal fence brackets

Chalk line measured from top of post shows you where to place the rail

Fit the rails by holding them in place and marking cut lines where the rail meets the posts

NAILING TECHNIQUE

Toenailing

Then, when you attach the rails, line the marks up with each other.

■ Predrill holes for fasteners and toenail the top rails to the posts with 10d nails, 3½-inch galvanized or treated screws, or rail hangers.

■ Then attach the bottom rails. When the frame is complete, remove any bracing that remains. Now you're ready to hang the infill.

BUILDING A FLAT-RAIL FRAME

You must build a flat-rail frame if your fence will have inset infill. Although building a flat-rail frame involves essentially the same techniques as for edge-rail framing, a few details demand additional attention:

■ First, because joints reduce the top rail's strength in tying the fence together along its length, you should minimize the number of joints by using top-rail stock long enough to span at least three posts.

■ Second, always butt top rails in the center of a post (right) so the surface will be wide enough for your fasteners.

Here's how to build the frame:

■ Distribute the rail material along the fence line to make the job go faster.

■ For fences built on level ground, predrill the long top-rail sections and fasten them to the posts with 10d nails or 3½-inch galvanized or treated screws. Then, measure (below), cut, and attach the remaining sections.

■ Measure, cut, and install the top and bottom rails for a stepped-frame fence one bay at a time.

■ Attach the bottom rails and kickboards. It's usually easier to install a center-mounted kickboard on the bottom rail before installing the rail. Fasten it to the rail with 3-inch screws every 8 to 10 inches. Toenail it to the posts at the ends.

■ If you're installing a side-mounted kickboard, cut it and nail or screw it to the bottom rail after the rail is installed.

■ If you're installing a cap rail, you can attach it at any time in the process (after the top rail, of course).

Nailing pattern at joints

Nailing pattern between joints

BUILDING A FLAT-RAIL FRAME

Posts cut level at top

Top rail

Kickboard

Bottom rails toenailed into place

SEEKING ITS OWN LEVEL

A commercial water level is a length of hose with clear plastic tubing fastened to each end. It is especially useful in fence construction because water finds its own level—over long distances and around obstacles.

Make your own from clear vinyl tubing. Fill it with colored water (use food coloring). Store the level with its ends plugged with rubber stoppers; or empty it, roll it up, and refill it for use later.

Bottom rail propped up for cutting

Marks for rail measured down from top of post

Bottom rail

Toenails

Kickboard

INSTALLING INFILL

HANGING SURFACE-MOUNTED INFILL

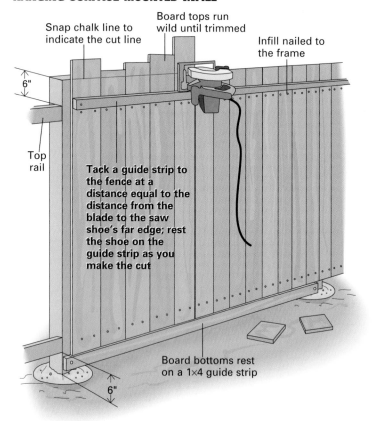

Snap chalk line to indicate the cut line

Board tops run wild until trimmed

Infill nailed to the frame

6"

Top rail

Tack a guide strip to the fence at a distance equal to the distance from the blade to the saw shoe's far edge; rest the shoe on the guide strip as you make the cut

Board bottoms rest on a 1×4 guide strip

6"

Now you're ready for the best part of fence building. It's here that your design—once only an idea—takes its final form. No matter how many boards you have to hang, nails to nail, or screws to screw, infill seems to go up fast. Perhaps that's because the end is now in sight, and since the process is repetitive, you can build up a rhythm that makes the work go faster.

Start by looking at infill in its two broadest categories: surface-mounted and inset.

Read about both processes, then look at the tips, techniques, and instructions for specific infill styles (see pages 58–67). Becoming familiar with this information beforehand will help you install your fence more easily.

SURFACE-MOUNTED INFILL

Surface-mounted infill requires less measuring and fitting, so fences built this way go up faster and easier than those with inset infill. You don't even need to precut boards to length for surface-mounted infill when fencing on level ground and with square-cut tops; you can let the board tops run wild—at random heights—and then cut them to a

finished line all at once. Infill boards finished with a cut top—pickets, points, or dog ears, for example—must be cut to size before you put them up. Here's how to install surface-mounted infill:

■ Distribute the materials along the fence line so they're close at hand.

■ Tack 1×3 or 1×4 boards to the posts along the bottom of the fence, spanning at least three bays (see the illustration at left). This board will serve as a guide to keep the bottom of the infill at a consistent height above the ground. (You can stretch a mason's line as a guide, but a board allows you set the infill directly on it—it's like having a third hand.) Level the guide if the ground is level; let it follow the slope for a contoured fence on evenly sloped terrain.

If you're building a contoured fence over uneven ground with variable slopes, a guide may be difficult to use. Instead, line up each board—by eye—with the bottom of the previous one.

■ Begin placing the infill at an end, corner, or gate post. Attach 1× stock with 8d nails or 2-inch treated screws; hang thinner material with 6d nails or 1½-inch screws.

If your fasteners are less than 2 inches from the top of the infill boards, predrill holes to keep the infill from splitting. Fasteners 2 inches or more from the top of the infill are less likely to split the wood, but it's still wise to drill pilot holes.

■ Check the leading edge of the infill with a carpenter's level every 3 or 4 feet to make sure it is plumb. (A spacer, as shown on page 58, can help keep the boards straight.) If the infill goes out of plumb, remove it and correct the problem—it's easier in the long run to fix a mistake early than to try adjusting subsequent boards to make it even.

■ Mark the finished height of the completed infill at both ends of the fence. Snap a chalk line between the marks, and trim the infill along the line.

To cut it quickly and accurately with a circular saw, measure down from the chalk line a distance equal to the the distance from your circular saw's blade to the edge of its soleplate. Tack a guide to the fence (see above left), and trim the infill. Watch out for uneven joints; they will catch the saw.

■ If you are staining or painting the fence and didn't do so before installation (see page 71) prepare the surfaces according to the finish manufacturer's instructions and apply the finish. Protect your landscaping and plantings with plastic tarps.

INSET INFILL

Inset infill requires more exacting construction, but produces clean lines and shows an equally attractive face on both sides. Here's how to install inset infill in a flat-rail frame.

■ Measure the dimensions of each bay. Unless all the bays are the same size—which is not likely—plan to cut and install the infill one bay at a time.

■ Check each bay for square. To check it, you can gauge each corner with a framing square or measure the diagonals. (If both diagonals are equal, the opening is square.)

You can usually work around minor out-of-square conditions as you install the infill. Wide stops, for example, can hide gaps. And you can cut sheet materials to fit exactly. Bays that are far out of square should be rebuilt.

■ Mark the position of the stops that are appropriate to the style of fence you've chosen. (Louvers will not require stops—see page 60.) Draw layout lines on both the posts and rails.

■ Cut the stops and infill boards to length. Determine whether you want mitered or butted stop joints, as shown in the detail illustrations below.

■ Fasten the stops into one side of the bay opening with either 6d or 8d finishing nails, depending on the thickness of the stops.

■ Working from the open side, fit the infill into the frame. Toenail the infill to the rails, not to the stops. Check for plumb as you go.

■ Fasten the other set of stops to the frame if required for your style of fence.

■ Prepare and finish the surfaces, protecting the landscaping with plastic tarps. Clean up the debris.

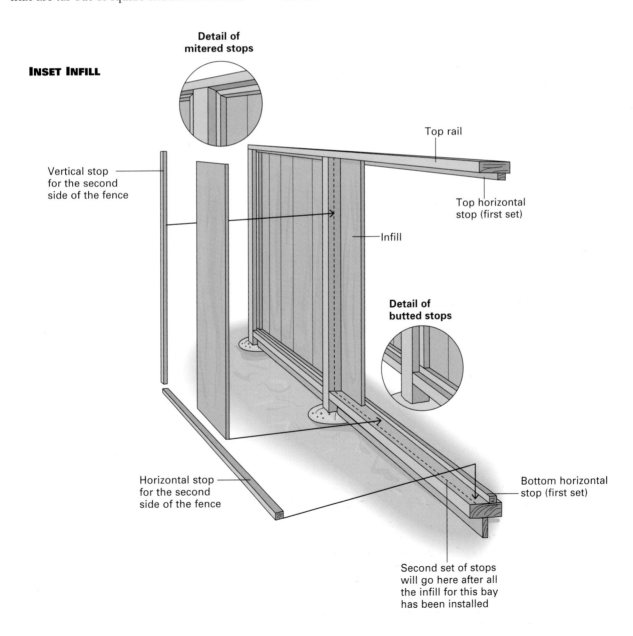

INSET INFILL

Detail of mitered stops

Top rail

Vertical stop for the second side of the fence

Top horizontal stop (first set)

Infill

Detail of butted stops

Horizontal stop for the second side of the fence

Bottom horizontal stop (first set)

Second set of stops will go here after all the infill for this bay has been installed

INSTALLING INFILL

continued

INFILL INSTALLATION TIPS

SPACING THE INFILL

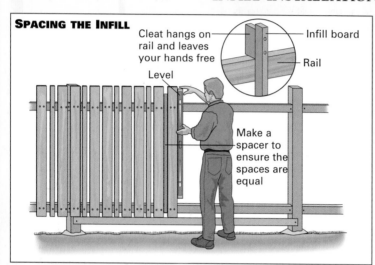

Cleat hangs on rail and leaves your hands free

Level

Infill board

Rail

Make a spacer to ensure the spaces are equal

CUTTING ANGLED INFILL

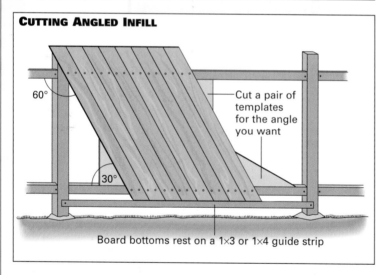

60°

30°

Cut a pair of templates for the angle you want

Board bottoms rest on a 1×3 or 1×4 guide strip

INSTALLING A KICKBOARD

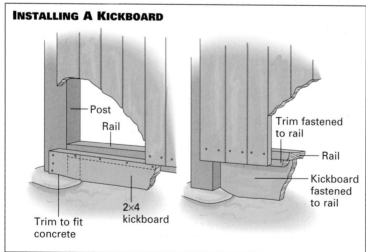

Post

Rail

Trim to fit concrete

2×4 kickboard

Trim fastened to rail

Rail

Kickboard fastened to rail

Whether your fence incorporates surface-mounted or inset infill, these tips will make fence building easier and result in a sturdier, better-looking job.

■ Don't scrimp on fasteners—either in quality or quantity. Galvanized or treated nails or screws cost slightly more but will last longer and stain the fence less than plain steel. Stainless-steel fasteners are the best choice. In addition to their own weight, fences have to carry extra loads imposed by rain, snow, wind, and climbing kids. Much of this stress falls on the fasteners—use plenty of them.

■ Hang boards plumb. Check the infill as you go—every few feet at least—with a 4-foot level (smaller levels may not be as accurate). If the infill has gotten out of plumb, take your work apart and correct it.

■ Equalize the spaces between pieces of infill. Make them regular with a cleated spacer; it will save you from measuring for each piece. Hang the cleat on the top rail so you can free both hands to hold the infill as you fasten it.

■ Keep angled infill even. Use a bevel square or make templates to properly position angled infill onto the frame.

■ Make bottom edges flush and smooth. Use guide boards to help place the infill (tack a 1×3 or 1×4 to the surface of the posts), unless your design intentionally calls for a random lengths. Reposition the guide every few bays as you work your way down the line.

■ To finish a wild-top edge, chalk a line at the cutting height. Then tack a 1×3 or 1×4 guide so a circular saw's soleplate can ride on it. Set the blade deep enough to cut through the infill, but no deeper. Rest the saw on the cutting guide and cut the entire top of the fence in one pass.

■ Install kickboards. Kickboards will close the gap under the bottom rail, providing a more finished look, and will keep animals from crawling under the fence. They also keep flat rails from sagging. Overlay them on the posts or inset them under the bottom rail; trim with a 1×2 if you want. Make the kickboard of pressure-treated lumber, heartwood, or a decay-resistant species like cedar or cypress because the board touches the earth and is subject to rot.

CONSTRUCTING CURVED FENCES

Curved fence sections can solve big problems in your landscape: They can skirt trees and other obstructions or soften corners where you want to avoid feeling cramped. And even if you don't have a specific problem to solve, curves add interest to your fence line.

They have their limitations, however. They're difficult to construct with between-post spans shorter than 4 feet or longer than 6 feet, they need at least three posts, and the infill has to be narrow, especially in tight curves.

To add a curved section, first lay it out (see page 49). With the posts set, follow the directions below to install the rails, either curved or a segmented. Hang the infill as you would on a straight rail.

CONTINUOUS CURVES

If you built the straight sections of your fence with flush-mounted rails, your curved section will have to follow suit. The best solution is to set the curved rails into dadoes in the posts. If your straight rails are face-mounted, your curved rails should be, too.

In either case, make the rails from layers of thinner stock rather than solid 2×4s. For deep arcs (tight curves), use four layers of ⅜-inch-thick redwood or two layers of 1×4 redwood with ¼-inch-deep saw kerfs spaced 1½ to 2 inches across the back. Unkerfed 1×4 redwood works well for shallower bends.

Soak the rails in water to make them more pliable. Fasten the first rail layer to the posts (or into 3½×1½-inch dadoes in them) with 2-inch screws. (Kerfs go to the inside of the curve.) Butt-join successive pieces at the center of a post.

Cut the board for the next layer to a different length so it will meet the next piece on a different post. Fasten this layer atop the first with screws long enough to go into the post through both layers. Use the same sequence to install the last two layers for a four-layer rail.

SEGMENTED RAILS

Segmented rails don't form a smooth curve, but cutting and installing them is easier than making curved rails.

To start, determine the miter-cut angle for the rail ends. You can calculate the angle mathematically, but it's much easier to lay it out graphically. To do so, hold a short piece of rail material between two posts. Align it along the rail axis, and bring the corner of one end up to the post face. To mark the angle, draw a line across the rail edge parallel to the post face. Cut the angle, and use the piece as a template to mark other rail ends or as a gauge to set your saw's bevel angle.

If you want to do the math, double the radius of your arc and multiply that number by 3.14 to find the arc's circumference. Divide the circumference by the distance between posts, then divide the resulting number into 360 degrees. The answer is your miter angle.

Cut the rails to fit between the posts for flush-mounted rails, as shown in the upper illustration below. Install them as shown at the bottom of the page to match surface-mounted rails.

Two layers of 1×4 redwood for rails

1×6 or 1×4 infill

Curved section requires three 4×4 posts

Rails dadoed into posts

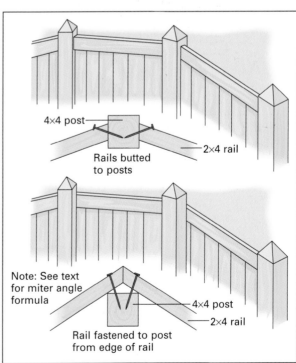

4×4 post

2×4 rail

Rails butted to posts

Note: See text for miter angle formula

4×4 post

2×4 rail

Rail fastened to post from edge of rail

SPECIFIC INFILL TECHNIQUES

BASKET WEAVE

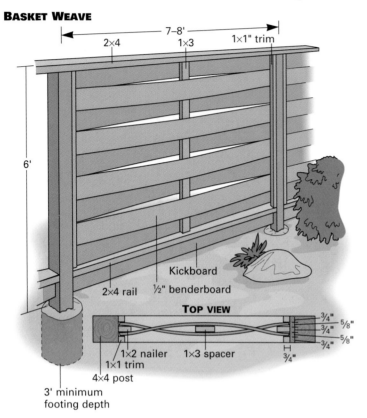

7–8'

2×4   1×3   1×1" trim

6'

Kickboard
½" benderboard

2×4 rail

TOP VIEW

¾"   ⅝"
¾"   ⅝"
¾"   ⅝"
¾"

1×2 nailer   1×3 spacer
1×1 trim
4×4 post

3' minimum
footing depth

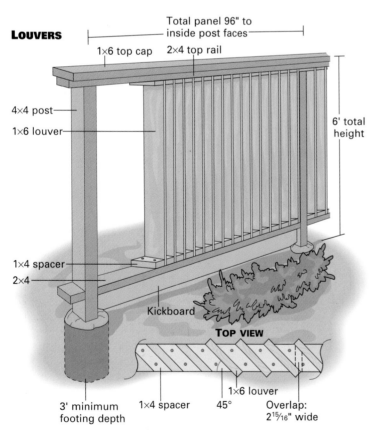

LOUVERS

Total panel 96" to
inside post faces

1×6 top cap   2×4 top rail

4×4 post

1×6 louver

6' total
height

1×4 spacer
2×4

Kickboard

TOP VIEW

1×6 louver

3' minimum   1×4 spacer   45°   Overlap:
footing depth   2¹⁵⁄₁₆" wide

BASKET WEAVE

Basket-weave infill, an inset style, calls for a flat-rail frame. Because the basket-weave boards add lateral strength to the frame, you may not need a kickboard for rail support. You can add one for appearance, however. Redwood ½×4 or ½×6-inch benderboard makes an ideal infill.

Space the 4×4 posts from 6 to 8 feet apart. Center a 1×2 nailer on each post and attach it with 8d finishing nails. Toenail a 1×3 or 1×2 spacer to the rails midway between the posts. You will weave the infill around this spacer and on either side of the post nailers.

Have someone hold one end of an infill board snugly against the nailer on one post, wind the trial piece around the vertical spacer, and mark the other end. Cut all the infill boards for the bay to this length.

Fasten the board to the nailers at each end with 6d or 8d box nails (angle them into the post faces). When you're done weaving and nailing, add trim made from mitered 1×1 stock around the inside of the bay.

LOUVERS

Install vertical or horizontal louvers as inset infill in a flat-rail frame (*pages 55 and 57*). Include a kickboard on a vertical-louver fence. Space the posts from 5 to 8 feet apart for vertical louvers, 4 to 6 feet for horizontal ones (longer horizontals may sag).

Unlike other inset infill, louvers don't require nailers; they do need spacers. Here's how to install louvered infill.

Measure the interior height (or the width for horizontal louvers) of the bay. Measure one bay at a time in case there's a slight difference from one to the other. Cut the 1×6 louver stock to length.

With a combination square, mark the position of the first louver at 45 degrees on the bottom and top rail. The corner of the louver should fit snugly against the post face.

Cut four triangular corner spacers to fit between the louver and the post on the top and bottom rails at each end of the bay. Cut a set of parallelograms (*left*) for the spacers between the louvers.

Toenail the first louver to the bottom rail and fasten it through the top rail. Face-nail the remaining spacers and louvers. You can vary the spacing and the angle of the louvers, but the design shown here, with 24 louvers, will fit neatly between posts with interior faces (not their centers) spaced 8 feet apart.

PICKETS

Pickets work equally well on edge-rail or flat-rail frames. The fence shown at right features flush-mounted edge rails. Flat rails would require a kickboard to minimize sagging.

Before you put up a picket fence, experiment with picket widths and spacing to get the look you want. Traditional 1×3 or 1×4 pickets spaced 2½ to 3 inches apart will give you a classic look, but there's a lot of leeway within those guidelines. To experiment with the possibilities, draw your ideas to scale on ¼-inch graph paper.

First establish your bay width—6 to 8 feet is ideal. Then, to figure the picket spacing, decide how many pickets you want to spread across the bay. Multiply that number by the actual picket width and subtract the result from the bay width to find total amount of space. Divide this figure by a number one more than the number of pickets to find the distance between pickets.

Cut a spacer jig to this width and fasten a cleat to it at a point that will put the top of the spacer at the shoulder of the picket (*right*).

Hang the spacer on the top rail as you install the pickets. Place the pickets so the bottoms fall about 2 inches above grade. Secure them to the rails with two 2¼-inch screws per picket.

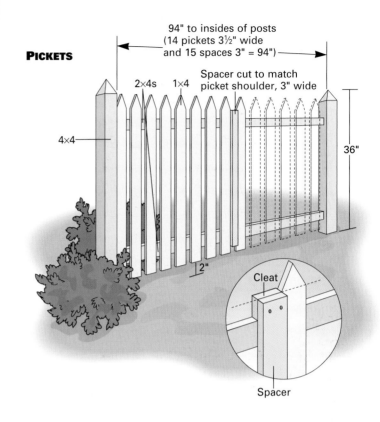

PICKETS

94" to insides of posts
(14 pickets 3½" wide
and 15 spaces 3" = 94")

2×4s   1×4

Spacer cut to match
picket shoulder, 3" wide

4×4

36"

2"

Cleat

Spacer

CUTTING A CURVED TOP

A scalloped top is a traditional decorative touch for a picket fence. It usually looks better with pickets closer together than the normal 2½ to 3 inches. Experiment with the spacing and picket width before you install the pickets. A good place to start is with spacing equal to half the picket width.

Let the tops run uneven as you install the pickets, but keep the bottoms about 2 inches off the ground. Use a spacing jig for uniformity.

Lay out the curve with a length of rope or decorator's cord about a foot longer than the span. Tack one end of it to the center of the picket or post at which the scallop will begin. Drape the other end over a nail at the opposite end of the scallop.

Move the free end of the cord to adjust the curve. The bottom of the curve should come to rest at least 1½ inches above the rail.

When the shape looks right to you, mark the cord and pencil the curve on the face of the pickets. Tape the rope in place to help with the tracing. Remove the rope, but mark the ends of the curve on the rope so you can duplicate the shape on the next bay.

Cut the pickets along the marked line with a saber saw. Sand the tops smooth.

1×4   4×4

Rope   1¾" space

SPECIFIC INFILL TECHNIQUES
continued

POST AND RAIL

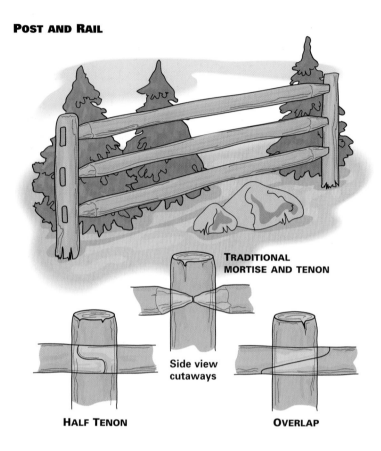

TRADITIONAL MORTISE AND TENON

Side view cutaways

HALF TENON

OVERLAP

DADOED POSTS

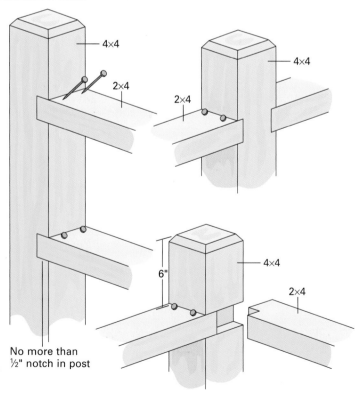

4×4

2×4

2×4

4×4

4×4

2×4

4×4

6"

2×4

No more than ½" notch in post

(See page 63 for information about cutting mortises.)

Post-and-rail fences look deceptively easy to assemble. If you start from scratch, cutting your own mortises and tenons, the rustic look allows you a certain amount of leeway in the name of hand-hewn craftsmanship.

You can purchase precut post-and-rail materials from lumberyards and home centers. Rails come in lengths of 6 to 10 feet and may be square (sawn rails) or wedge-shaped (split). And, of course, you can buy raw logs and make your own.

Lay out your fence line and dig the postholes, but don't set the posts until you cut the mortises in them. (See page 63 for information about cutting mortises.)

Measure the tenons on the rail ends. If you are working with raw stock, form the tenons first, then mortise the posts to fit them. Cut the tenon shoulders with a saw, then form the tenon itself by sawing, chiseling, or planing the waste away.

For rustic fences, cut mortises ⅛ to ¼ inch larger than the tenons; for more formal fences built of milled lumber, cut the mortises to fit the tenons exactly. Measure down from the top of the post to mark each mortise location so the mortises are in the same place on all posts. You should be able to locate the top rail 2 to 6 inches from the top of the post and the bottom one 6 to 8 inches from the bottom, with the middle rail centered between them.

Board and dimensioned-lumber rails require fixed height posts, and rustic rail fences on level ground will look better with them also. Set them according to the directions on page 53, starting at a corner with the first post firmly in its footing. Set the next post loosely, and insert the rails in both. Then pour the second footing and proceed down the fence line, one bay at a time.

DADOED POSTS

Construct dadoed fences with boards (1× material) or dimension-lumber (2× stock) for rails. Unlike their rustic mortised counterparts, dadoed fences do not span irregular terrain well. Their precise joints must fit squarely, so they don't allow for much give to adjust to grades.

Lay out your fence and dig the postholes as described on page 52.

Mark locations for the dadoes on the posts, measuring from the top for uniformity. Cut the dadoes as shown on page 63.

Set the posts following the procedure shown for fixed-height posts on page 53. Fasten the rails to the posts, completing one bay at a time. Predrill pilot holes, and secure the rails with rustproof screws.

DADOES AND MORTISES

Dadoes and mortises increase the strength of fencing joints and enhance their aesthetic appeal. If you haven't cut them before, you'll find the skill easy to acquire (take a few practice cuts on scrap). Make sure your cutting tools are sharp. Sharp tools are safer than dull tools and produce better looking—and better fitting—joints.

CUTTING DADOES

First, mark the outline of the dado to be cut. Most dadoes are cut exactly opposite one another on the same post. It's usually more efficient to line up several posts at once, clamp them to a working surface, and use a framing square to mark the edges of the dado on all the surfaces. Whether working on one post or many, always measure down from the top of the stock you are cutting.

Use a circular saw or backsaw to cut the kerfs within the dado outline. If you've marked several posts at the same time and are cutting with a circular saw, leave the posts in place and clamp a 1×3 guide to keep the saw plate straight. If you're cutting with a backsaw, clamp a guide to the blade at the depth of the cut.

Make several cuts with your saw, each about ¼ inch from the previous one, and all of them to the same depth, It will be difficult to cut the waste cleanly if the kerfs are at different depths. A dado in a 4×4 post should usually be cut no more than ½ inch deep. Cutting deeper will compromise the strength of the post.

Remove the waste with a sharp chisel, keeping the bevel toward the wood and tapping the handle with a mallet. Make the dado sides and bottom clean and flat.

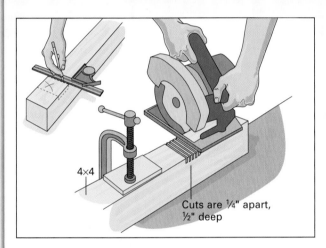

4×4

Cuts are ¼" apart, ½" deep

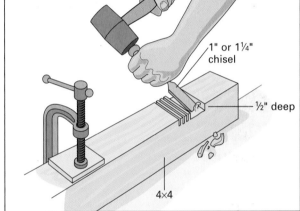

1" or 1¼" chisel

½" deep

4×4

CUTTING MORTISES

Mortises, like dadoes, must be cut in the same location on each post. Measure down from the top of each post so all the mortises begin in the same height.

First, mark the outline of the mortise on the surface of the post. Use a piece of scrap with the same dimensions as the rail or use a cardboard template cut to the same size.

Next, use a ½- to ¾-inch spade bit and drill out the center of the mortise outline. Position your bit so the edge cuts along the edge of your outline.

The last step is to clean out the sides of the mortise with a sharp chisel. Tap gently with a mallet and keep the bevel of the chisel facing the wood. Gently smooth the surface with the flat side of the chisel.

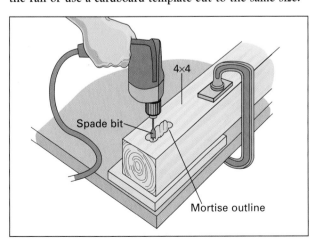

4×4

Spade bit

Mortise outline

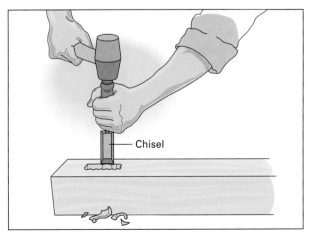

Chisel

SPECIFIC INFILL TECHNIQUES

continued

CLAPBOARD

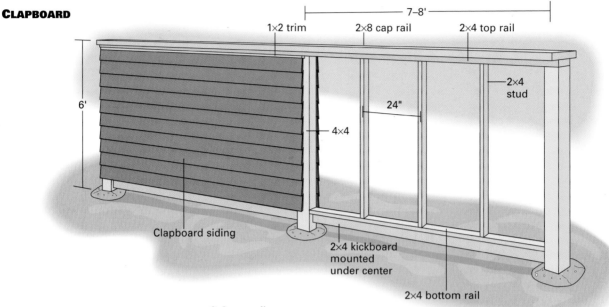

Labels: 7–8'; 1×2 trim; 2×8 cap rail; 2×4 top rail; 6'; 2×4 stud; 24"; 4×4; Clapboard siding; 2×4 kickboard mounted under center; 2×4 bottom rail

SHINGLES

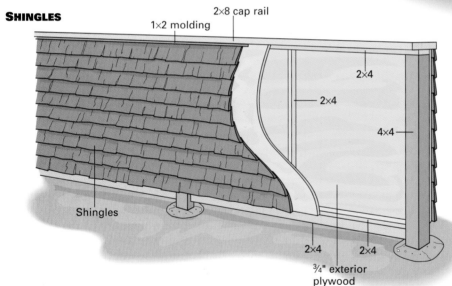

Labels: 2×8 cap rail; 1×2 molding; 2×4; 2×4; 4×4; Shingles; 2×4; 2×4; ¾" exterior plywood

SIDING FENCES

When you're building a siding fence, you're essentially building a free-standing exterior wall on the infill.

Start by setting your posts at least 3 feet into the ground to carry the heavy weight of this fence. Don't be concerned with aesthetics when spacing your posts because they are less visible in this design. Post spacing of 8 feet will work well with most materials.

Next, build a flat-rail frame (see page 55) and toenail 2×4 studs to the top and bottom rails every 16 or 24 inches. Use pressure-treated lumber throughout the frame—the cavity between the exterior and interior faces of the fence will trap moisture so you need rot-resistant framing.

CLAPBOARD OR HARDBOARD: Nail a starter strip (as thick as the bottom edge of the siding) along the bottom of the frame. Then, working upwards, fasten the siding to the posts and studs with 8d galvanized nails. If you're not going to paint the fence, use aluminum siding nails.

SHINGLES: Cover the frame with ¾-inch plywood sheathing or nail 1×4 horizontal furring strips to the studs, spacing them at the length of the shingles (generally 15 to 18 inches). Fasten the shingles with 3d galvanized or aluminum box nails (two per shingle, ¾ inch from edges). Space the shingles ⅛ inch apart and stagger the overlaps 1½ inches. To keep the courses straight, snap a chalk line across each row at the point where the next course will begin.

OTHER MATERIALS: For Dolly Varden, beveled, or shiplap siding, install the infill without a starter strip. Attach with 8d casing nails. Tongue-and-groove siding looks better installed as panel fencing. (See page 65.)

In most settings and with most materials, a 1×8 cap rail enhances the appearance of a siding-covered fence.

PANEL INSERTS

2×6 cap rail

2×4

Stop

4×4

Stop

PANEL INFILL

Although you can surface-mount panel infill, it presents far more design options and presents a more finished appearance when you treat it as inset infill.

Build flat-rail framing (see page 55) with posts spaced appropriate to the material. Plywood panels work neatly with 8-foot spacing between the post faces (not the on-center spacing). Lattice and acrylic need more support—4- to 6-foot spacing is better.

Set posts 2 feet deep (or according to local codes). Next, attach the rails and toenail the internal 2×4 framing in place. Mark posts and rails for the position of the stops appropriate to the thickness of your infill (1×2s for ¾-inch plywood, lattice, and tongue-and-grooved siding, 2×2s for acrylic).

Attach one set of stops with 6d or 8d finishing nails. Next install the infill. Toenail plywood and lattice; for acrylic, precaulk the rail along the stop with silicone. For tongue-and-groove siding, toenail the sides and run a thin bead of polyurethane glue along the grooves as you set each piece. Finish by installing the other set of stops butted against the infill.

PREFABRICATED METAL

The metal fence installation shown here illustrates a typical assembly. With this type of fencing, however, you should always follow the manufacturer's instructions carefully when putting up your own fence.

First, set an end post in concrete. Let the concrete set up for just a few minutes, then adjust the height of the post so that it corresponds to the height of the fence panel and will put the panel the proper distance above the ground. Check the post for plumb with a carpenter's level on two adjacent sides (or with a post level), brace the post, and let the concrete set firmly.

Insert and fasten the mounting brackets into the rails and screw them to the first post. Then attach the panel loosely to the second post. Plumb the second post, then pour the concrete footing.

After the concrete sets for a few minutes, adjust the second post so it's plumb, making sure that the rail is level. Continue this process until you get to the final post. Then hang the gate with the brackets and fasteners included in the kit.

RAIL MOUNTING DETAIL

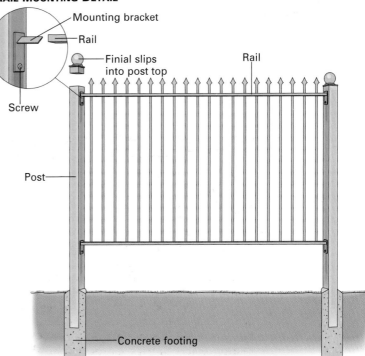

Mounting bracket

Rail

Finial slips into post top

Rail

Screw

Post

Concrete footing

SPECIFIC INFILL TECHNIQUES
continued

VINYL

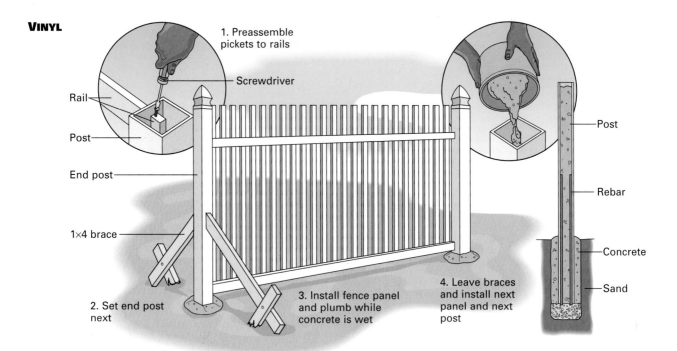

1. Preassemble pickets to rails

Screwdriver

Rail

Post

End post

1×4 brace

2. Set end post next

3. Install fence panel and plumb while concrete is wet

4. Leave braces and install next panel and next post

Post

Rebar

Concrete

Sand

VINYL FENCING

Vinyl fencing installs relatively easily, although it requires a few more steps due to the nature of the materials. Unlike other infill materials, the vinyl panels have to be assembled before you erect the fence. All the components come precut, so you won't be in doubt about where everything goes or in what order. Of course, you should always follow the manufacturer's directions.

To make the assembly easier, build a pair of 2×4 stands to hold the panel sections as you put them together. A few manufacturers furnish panels that require PVC cement for assembly. When gluing, make sure the parts are clean and that you have plenty of ventilation. Working outdoors is best.

After you've assembled the panels, lay out the fence line and dig the postholes. Instead of marking your layout line with tape, lay an assembled panel on the ground or hold it in place as a marker for the location of each successive hole. Most manufacturers recommend postholes 12 inches in diameter; proper depth varies with the height of the fence.

Instead of a gravel base in the hole, pour in about 4 inches of sand—you can easily push the post base into it so rainwater will drain out. Insert the first post and pour in concrete.

Depending on the fence style and manufacturer's instructions, either set the remaining posts at the same time, or set them panel by panel. In either case, fit the panel rails into the precut holes in the posts, secure them with PVC cement or the manufacturer's hardware, and adjust the posts so the panels are level and plumb. Brace them temporarily—tape the braces to the posts to keep them in place—until the concrete sets.

After the concrete has cured, strengthen the terminal posts with ½-inch rebar and concrete, as shown in the illustration. Tie mason's line to one end of the rebar and drop it into the post corners, fold the line back down the outside of the post to help keep the rebar in the corner, and pour in concrete from a small container. Pour at least to the top of the rebar (about half the post height). Better yet, fill the post with concrete—it will keep the water out.

For contoured installations, set the posts one panel at a time. Cut the rail ends at an angle (so they will clear the opposite rail inside the post) and enlarge the hole in the post to accommodate the angled rail. Rack each panel to conform to the contour, install it in the post, and adjust the post until the contour is correct and the post is plumb.

For stepped fencing, use an end post for every new fence level. End posts have one face uncut, and it's in that face that you will cut new holes at the level of your step-down. Cut holes in all your posts and install them as above, a panel at a time.

CHAIN LINK

Many people don't appreciate the value of chain-link fences. If you need a fence principally for security—around a swimming pool or to keep kids or pets in the yard—and you want a long-lasting, almost maintenance-free solution, you can hardly beat chain link.

Building a chain-link fence is not difficult, and you'll find all the materials to buy and the tools to rent at you local fence supplier.

Choose the width of your mesh (also called the fabric) in 4-foot, 5-foot, or 6-foot rolls. The mesh is woven from 6-gauge to 11-gauge galvanized steel (6-gauge is thicker, and thus stronger), and you can also find vinyl-coated fencing in a variety of colors. You also have a choice in the size of the mesh opening—wider is cheaper, but smaller is more difficult to climb. A maximum opening of 1¼ inches is recommended for swimming pool fences unless you insert wood or plastic slats.

Lay out the fence line and space the posts no more than 10 feet apart and set all the posts plumb in concrete (see pages 48 to 53). Terminal posts are larger than intermediate posts and require different fittings. Set terminal posts in 8-inch-diameter holes, 18 to 30 inches deep (depending of fence height and local codes).

Run a line between the terminal posts about 4 inches lower than the top and set the line posts to this height in 6-inch-diameter holes, 18 to 24 inches deep.

After the concrete has cured for several days, install the tension bands, end band, and a post cap on each of the terminal posts, and a loop cap on each of the intermediate posts. Thread the top rails carefully through the loop caps and into the end bands, using rail sleeves to join sections of rail.

Unroll the chain-link mesh along the outside of the fence and lean it against the posts. Slide a tension bar through the end row of mesh and secure it to the tension bands on one terminal post. Moving along the fence line, tie the mesh loosely to the top rail with tie wires.

Slide a stretching bar (or another tension bar) through the mesh about 3 or 4 feet from the next terminal post. Attach a fence stretcher (you can rent one) to the stretching bar and the terminal post, and tighten the mesh until you can squeeze an opening no more than about ½ inch. Cut the top and bottom links and unthread the surplus mesh, slide a tension bar through the end, and secure the tension bands to it. Tie the mesh to the top rail and posts.

To install the gate, first attach the fittings to the gate posts, then hang the gate on the hinges. Finally, set the gate latch.

INSTALLING A CHAIN-LINK FENCE

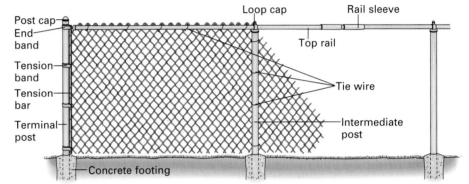

USING STRETCHING BAR

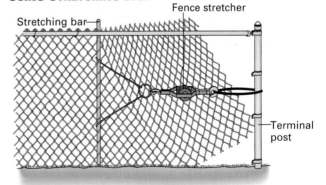

GATE INSTALLED

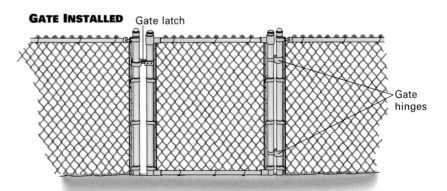

ADDITIONS AND REPAIRS

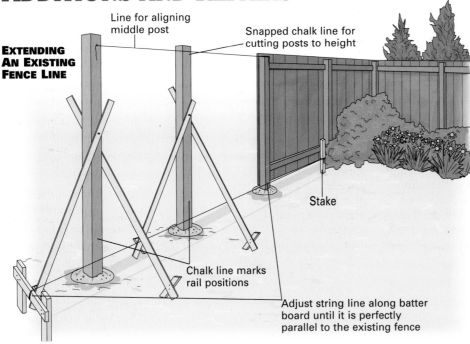

EXTENDING AN EXISTING FENCE LINE

Line for aligning middle post

Snapped chalk line for cutting posts to height

Stake

Chalk line marks rail positions

Adjust string line along batter board until it is perfectly parallel to the existing fence

Then, to make sure your fence gives you years of service in return for your effort and investment, give it a periodic check and make repairs promptly.

EXTEND A FENCE

Drive a stake 6 feet before the start of the existing fence and about 1 inch away from it. Set batter boards about 4 feet past the end of the new section.

Tie a line between these points, adjusting it until it's exactly parallel to the existing fence. Measure from the line to the center of the existing posts; with this measurement, mark the centers of your new holes. Dig the holes, readjust the line, and set the posts.

ADD A PERPENDICULAR SECTION

Start the new section at an existing post or set a new post for the addition and fasten it to a mullion attached to the old bay (see below left). Drive a batter board about 4 feet beyond the end of the new section. Stretch a line from the existing fence to the batter board. Square it, using the 3–4–5 triangle method (see page 49). Measure and mark your new post locations on the line, and transfer them to the ground. Dig the postholes, set the posts, and add the rails and infill as you would for new fencing.

It's easy to add new fencing to an existing fence—simply duplicate the dimensions and materials of the old section and install the new one, connecting it to the old one.

To minimize the brand-new look of your addition, apply a quick-weathering finish or stain that makes the new and old match more closely. If your fence is painted, repaint the old section when you paint the new one.

CONDUCT A FENCE CHECKUP

Fences can lose their structural strength in several ways. Posts rot and their footings crack, loosen, or give out because the fence wasn't properly aligned when built. Wood splits, nails loosen, and termites make your fence their home. To avoid trouble, check your fence yearly, looking for these problems.

ROT: For posts in concrete, poke around the base with an ice pick or screwdriver. For earth-and-gravel backfill, dig down about 6 inches. What you're looking for is soft or spongy wood. If you find it, it means rot has set in.

INSTALLING A PERPENDICULAR ADDITION

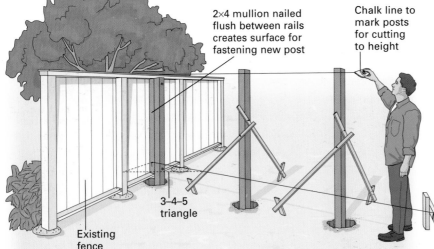

2×4 mullion nailed flush between rails creates surface for fastening new post

Chalk line to mark posts for cutting to height

3–4–5 triangle

Existing fence

Replace the post—it will gradually weaken the fence. Look for rot where the rails meet the infill or posts. Repair or replace anything that has rotted.

POSTS OUT OF PLUMB: If the posts aren't plumb, the fence won't be either. If posts begin to tilt, the forces of nature will loosen the rails until they and the infill eventually pull away. Realign and reset the posts; refasten the rails and the infill. Shrub and plant shoots can also force joints apart. Cut vigorous plants away from the fence and nail the joints that have worked loose.

SURFACE FINISH: Fences look better and wear longer when the finish repels moisture. If your fence is painted or stained, a recoat can add years to its life. If it has been treated with a sealer, drop some water on a horizontal section. If the water beads, the sealer is adequate. But if the wood absorbs the water, it's time to reapply the sealer.

FASTENERS: Over time, nails and screws can loosen. Inspect all the fasteners on the fence, and tighten any that are loose. If one won't stay in, try a larger nail or screw.

LOOSE POSTS: Drive pressure-treated shims into the post. In an earth-and-gravel backfill, nail the wedges to the post, then tamp the earth. In concrete, trim off the protruding shims, then run a bead of polyurethane caulk around the top. If a post in an earth-and-gravel footing is too loose, dig out the backfill and reset the post in concrete.

DECAYED POSTS: To mend a decayed post, first support the fence temporarily with blocks on both sides of the post. Then cut away the old post about 1 or 2 inches above grade or as close to that point as sound wood remains. Leave the rails and infill connected.

■ Dig a new posthole next to the footing. If the post was set with a concrete collar, break up the collar with a wrecking bar and remove it. If the post is set in a full concrete footing, remove the old footing. Wrestle it free and pull it out. If the post was set with earth-and-gravel backfill, dig it out.

■ Refill the old hole with soil and tamp it level with the surrounding grade.

■ Put 6 inches of gravel in the bottom of the new posthole. Cut a length of post (pressure-treated or heartwood of a decay-resistant species) so it will extend about 3 feet above the surface. Cut the top of it

at a 45-degree angle so it can shed water.

■ Place the post in the hole, work it several inches into the gravel bed, and mark bolt positions so that the lowest bolt is 6 to 8 inches above ground— higher if the wood isn't fully sound to that point.

■ Drill holes for ½-inch galvanized carriage bolts, and securely fasten the new and the old posts together. Plumb the fence. If it leans badly, work it back slowly with a winch and brace it.

■ Fill the hole with concrete and crown the top to shed water. After the concrete cures, remove the braces.

A LEANING FENCE: Fences often lean either because posts have rotted or because earth movement has forced the structure out of alignment. To reposition the fence and add new posts to support it, follow these steps:

■ Brace the leaning posts with 2×4s. Then dig out the earth next to the footings so you can pull the fence toward these recesses. Dig down at least two-thirds the depth of the footing. Don't remove rails or infill.

REPAIRING LOOSE POSTS

Pressure-treated shim nailed to post

Earth-and-gravel backfill

Cut shim at concrete

Polyurethane caulk

Concrete footing

MENDING DECAYED POSTS AND TRUING A LEANING FENCE

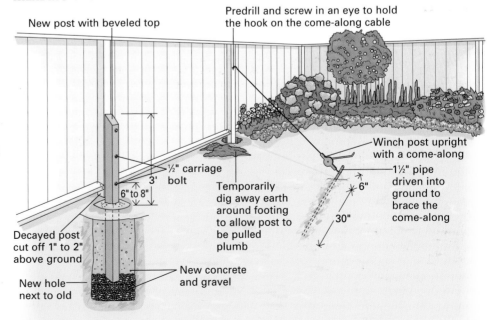

New post with beveled top

Predrill and screw in an eye to hold the hook on the come-along cable

½" carriage bolt

3'

6" to 8"

Decayed post cut off 1" to 2" above ground

New hole next to old

New concrete and gravel

Temporarily dig away earth around footing to allow post to be pulled plumb

Winch post upright with a come-along

1½" pipe driven into ground to brace the come-along

6"

30"

ADDITIONS AND REPAIRS

continued

ADDING A POST MIDSPAN

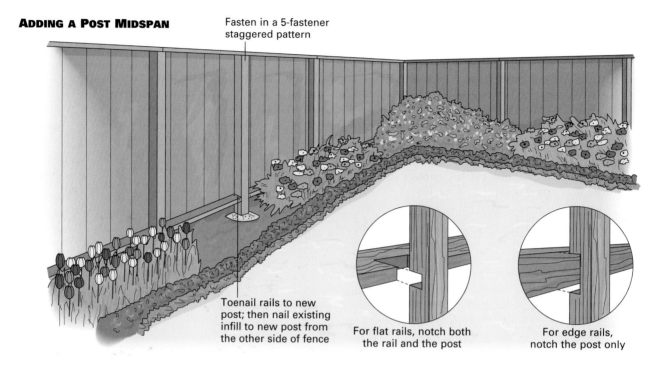

Fasten in a 5-fastener staggered pattern

Toenail rails to new post; then nail existing infill to new post from the other side of fence

For flat rails, notch both the rail and the post

For edge rails, notch the post only

REPAIRING RAILS

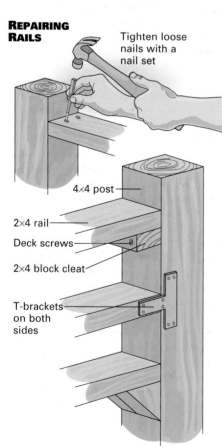

Tighten loose nails with a nail set

4×4 post

2×4 rail

Deck screws

2×4 block cleat

T-brackets on both sides

■ Predrill and twist a screw eye into each post about ⅔ up from the ground. Hook a come-along (you can rent this type of winch) into the eye and pull the fence back into alignment a little at a time. Winch a little at the end posts, then at the next posts, then the next, and back again, rebracing each amount of gain (see illustration, page 69).

■ When the fencing is upright and braced plumb, mark the on-center position for the new posts. They will be least noticeable at the exact center of each existing bay.

■ Measure and mark posthole locations, then dig them out with a clamshell digger. The posts will be notched (see the illustration above); place the holes so the posts will be centered and flush with the framework.

■ Shovel 6 inches of gravel into each hole.

Place each post in its hole and work it about 2 inches into the gravel. Make sure the post is plumb and mark the notches on both it and the rail.

■ Notch both the new post and the existing rail, and fasten them with rust-resistant screws. Check for plumb and rebrace the post if necessary.

■ When all posts are fastened and braced, fill the postholes with concrete and crown the footings with a slope so they shed water.

■ Wait until the concrete is fully cured (three days to a week), then remove the bracing and refasten any loose rails or infill that may have worked free. Don't use the same fastener holes. If the wood is dry, it may split, so drill pilot holes first, using a bit slightly smaller than the fastener's shank.

■ Stain or paint the new posts or give them quick-weathering treatment to make the repair less noticeable.

LOOSE RAILS: Loose or rotted rails can be repaired and reattached to posts. The illustration at left shows several simple ways to reattach a loose rail: Fasten a 2×4 cleat support under the rail, attach an angle bracket or T-plate to the post and rail, or cut two 2×4s at a 45-degree angle and fasten them side by side under the end. After repairing the joint, caulk it.

If the rot extends into the rail by more than the width of the new support, replace the entire rail.

SELECTING AND APPLYING FINISHES

People usually put a particular finish on a fence to achieve a particular look. Surface finishes do contribute to the look and style of a fence and can help blend it into your landscape. Finishes also provide the important function of protection. Keeping a fence properly finished can add years to its life. If it weren't for the weather, you wouldn't have to worry about the durability of your fence. But wind, rain, snow, ice, and sun exact a heavy toll on fences; the right finish can help protect your fence from damage and decay.

CHOOSING THE FINISH

Ask yourself how you want the fence to look. Do you want to paint it, stain it, or let it weather? With a clear finish, redwood and cedar show off their natural color. They also look well when left to weather. Most picket fences, however, seem made for paint—although weathered pickets complement woodland settings.

First consider color, tone, and surface sheen (flat or glossy). Then turn your attention to durability and ease of application. If you use one product along with another, make sure they're compatible. Your material supplier will be able to help you choose finishes.

SEALERS

Clear or lightly pigmented sealers—also called water repellents—seal wood against water penetration. They protect the wood, but don't change its appearance appreciably. A clear sealer may slow the graying of wood, but it will not stop it.

A wide range of additives increases the effectiveness of sealers. Some ward off mildew, insects, and fungi; ultraviolet blockers diminish the effect of the sun's rays and maintain the natural color of the wood.

Pigmented sealers can provide the same protection while slightly changing the color of the wood. All-purpose sealers usually contain water repellents, preservatives, and ultraviolet blockers.

You can apply sealers over or under stains and under primer and paint for extra protection.

PAINTS

Paints form an opaque film, so they can conceal some defects in lumber. Surfaces to be painted should be primed first. Painted finishes tend to last longer and look better on smooth surfaces than on rough ones. And, of course, they can be recoated.

Exterior alkyds (oil-based products) are costly, require solvents for cleanup, and dry slowly. Water-based latex paints don't cost as much as alkyds, clean up easily with water, and dry quickly. Both kinds come in a range of colors and sheens (gloss, semigloss, flat, or matte).

Oil-based primers provide better protection on raw wood than water-based primers. Add stain blockers to stop bleed-through from redwood and cedar. A good-quality acrylic-latex top coat applied over an alkyd primer is probably the most durable and protective fence finish.

STAINS

Stains change the look of a surface, but most offer little protection. Stains are somewhat less expensive than paints, and application goes faster than painting because stains don't require an undercoat. They go on easily over rough or smooth surfaces. Apply oil-based stains on redwood and red cedar.

Semitransparent stains allow more of the wood's grain to show through than do heavy-bodied stains, but they wear away more quickly. They are particularly suitable for highlighting the beauty of wood grains. Heavy-bodied stains contain more pigments and hide the grain more.

No matter what their pigment level, stains don't offer much variation in sheen; they tend to retain the wood's low-luster, natural look.

BLEACHING TREATMENTS, WEATHERING STAINS

Bleaching treatments don't protect the wood at all, but they change its appearance by lightening its natural tones. Bleaching treatments offer an intermediate solution to the problem of toning down the jarring look of a brand-new fence. They soften the raw wood look and help fence materials blend in quickly. You get the effect of two seasons of natural weathering in one application, because, like the sun, the treatments strip color from the wood fibers. Some products are harmful to plants and grasses.

Sealers stop the bleach from working. So, if you plan to bleach the wood, don't seal it first. Wait two months after applying the bleach to seal the wood.

APPLYING THE FINISH

If you're building a new fence, apply the finish before you build it. That way, you're protecting all the surfaces. But if you want to wait until you have installed the fence, take these steps. Before applying the finish, read the manufacturer's instructions.

Let the wood dry for a few weeks, so it's more absorbent. For best results, give the entire fence a good cleaning. Scrub the fence with a moderately stiff brush and a solution of 1 cup household chlorine bleach and 1 gallon water, then rinse it well. If the fence has weathered naturally for some time and you would like to restore the original wood color, use 1 part bleach with 3 parts water, or a deck cleaner. Protect plantings along the fence line.

You can apply most finishes with a brush, pad, roller, or sprayer. For larger projects use an airless sprayer, but practice spraying on scrap wood first. Apply sealers with a good-quality roller that has a 1-inch nap. You can recoat most clear sealers while they are still wet.

BUILDING GATES

Gates give your fence the finishing touch. Whether a gate blends into the fence, like the ones at right and below, or becomes a landscape feature in itself, like the one at left, it calls for careful planning and construction.

Although a gate might seem an undemanding structure at first glance, it routinely endures loads and stresses that require strong joints and hefty hardware. Remember swinging on a gate as a youngster?

This chapter will help you plan what gates you need—their locations, width, direction of swing, and other attributes. Then, it will show you the techniques for building and installing sturdy, smooth-swinging gates that will finish your fence project perfectly.

Scalloped tops make the gates in this low fence seem even lower.

At first, you may not notice that this fence section is really a gate. By repeating elements of the fence bays in the gate and its frame, the homeowners have created an understated entrance to this garden.

DESIGNING GATES

Massive hinges add to the character of these redwood gates. They carry the high style of the redwood fence across the driveway, lending continuity to the home and yard.

On one level, a gate serves simply to open or close a gap in the fence. On a deeper level, however, gates serve much more complicated—and aesthetic—purposes. Gates make statements about the occupants of a property and the landscape to which they permit entrance. They can function as focal points and punctuate the entry, or highlight some special area on the site.

FIRST IMPRESSIONS

Gates create an image, project an impression, and offer signals about how they should be approached and about what lies beyond.

A tall locked gate does not invite entrance, except to one who holds the key. Low, painted pickets, on the other hand, let those who approach know they're welcome, especially if they open on to a path in bloom.

Some gates seem destined to stand open; others look imperious, as if you should state your business before passing through. And while a few gates are strictly utilitarian, others can be exuberantly whimsical and fantastic.

Although a gate may be the last element you will actually build in the fence, don't wait until you've completed the fence before designing your gate. At a minimum, you should decide three things about the gate or gates before you finalize your fence line: location, size, and direction of swing.

Rely on common sense when picking the gate's location. It should be convenient and fall on natural traffic paths. Determine the size of the gate by what will pass through it (See *Guidelines for Gate Openings* on page 77), and note that the direction of its swing depends on where you place it (see page 76).

Then, keep your overall fence style—and the following pointers—in mind as you begin to make decisions about the appearance of your gate.

A GATE AS A STRUCTURAL SYSTEM

Gates, like fences, form a structural system unto themselves. Regardless of style, each gate is composed of framing, infill, and sometimes bracing. The strength of a gate depends on its structural design as well as the quality of its materials and construction.

Gates place a heavy load on their fences, and gateposts are typically larger and are set deeper than intermediate posts.

To join the parts of the system together, install hardware that is of the appropriate size and also matches the style of the fence. Latches, catches, hinges, and other accessories function more than mechanically. They are as much a part of the aesthetics of a gate as the gate itself.

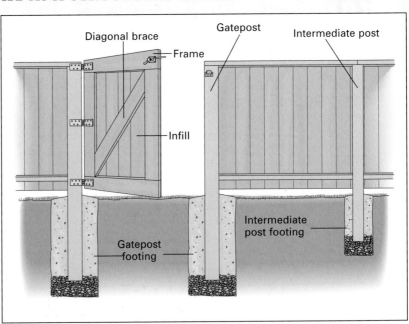

Diagonal brace

Gatepost

Intermediate post

Frame

Infill

Gatepost footing

Intermediate post footing

■ **CONTRAST:** Contrast calls attention to a gate; a gate that's different from the fence around it gets noticed. You can create a contrast in your gate by building it from different materials (tubular metal on a wood fence, for example) or by using the same materials in a different way.

■ **COMPLEMENT:** A gate that matches the fence, detail for detail, effectively disappears from view. Make your gate match the fence when you want to downplay its appearance or enhance privacy. To make it less apparent, hinge the gate frame so it's flush with the fence surface.

■ **COMBINATION:** A gate that harmonizes with the style of the fence but incorporates special effects—such as an open top or distinguishing trim— invites attention to itself without detracting from the visual continuity of the fence line. An arbor or canopy further sets off an entry.

Gridded panels atop the fence echo in the gates. The curved tops effectively lower the height, making the gates appear less forbidding. The pergola with a light calls even more attention to the entry which, though massive, seems welcoming. The redwood has been painted for a lighter look.

FUNCTION AND MATERIALS

Depending on its purpose, one of your gates may require more visual predominance than another. A main-entry gate, for instance, deserves a more prominent design than one leading into a service yard. How you achieve that effect for your gate depends largely on materials and how you combine them.

A metal gate hung on an ornamental metal fence makes a lasting and attractive combination. So does a wood gate on a wood fence, whether you hang a prefabricated model or design one yourself. However, a metal gate in a wood fence will look best on a solid-surfaced board fence or on one with a simple, straight-lined style.

If you've counted on a metal gate but can't afford ornamental iron, don't give up. Look at prefabricated metal gate styles. Appearance, quality, and price vary according to the gauge and type of metal and the size and design of the gate.

Lattice-topped panels flanking the gate set it apart from the redwood fence while the gate itself reflects the design of the fence bays. Also, the gate stands taller than the fence, adding to the entranceway's sense of importance.

DESIGNING GATES
continued

DESIGNING THE GATE

Planning a gate requires careful thought; building it demands precision. Successful gates function smoothly and look good, even in their old age. For a gate to do its job well, these three elements must work together:

THE STRUCTURE: Adequate framing and bracing, solid joints, and securely fastened infill make a durable gate. Poor-quality materials or faulty construction will quickly doom a gate. A gate that's too wide to support itself will sag, and an overly heavy one can put an unnecessary—and often damaging—burden on the hardware.

THE HARDWARE: Rustproof fasteners—stainless-steel screws are the best—plus stout hinges, latches, catches, and locks are necessities for a gate's proper function, appearance, and durability. Buy hardware, especially hinges, adequate for the size and weight of your gate. Attach the hardware securely with screws.

THE GATEPOSTS: Gateposts must be set sufficiently deep in stable footings to transfer the load of the gate to the ground. Because gateposts must both support the weight of the gate and withstand the forces of opening and closing, they are often one size larger than the intermediate fence posts.

As you design your gate, leave decisions about style, infill, and special details until last. You can mount almost any kind of infill to create the look you want. Plan the structure first, beginning with this question: How wide should the gate be?

THE WIDTH OF THE OPENING

If a gate is too wide, you'll soon find it sagging and out of square because of its own weight. Tradition says that 4 feet is about the limit for a commonly hinged, one-panel, unsupported gate.

If the fence opening must be wider than 4 feet, you have two options: span the opening with a pair of panels or with a single gate into which you've built extra support—a wheel or a diagonally mounted turnbuckle. (See *Guidelines for Gate Openings,* page 77.)

THE SWING OF THE GATE

To determine which way your gate should swing, look at its surroundings. These illustrations show how the conditions at the location of the gate affect the direction that it

can swing. Your gate may be able to swing open in both directions. If so, you can purchase special hardware for it. (See pages 80 and 81 for an overview of hardware styles.)

Here are some of the more common gate locations and how they affect the swing of the gate:

BOUNDARY-LINE FENCES: Gates installed at property edges are usually mounted so they swing into the property. Don't rule out hinging a gate to swing both ways, however, especially if the gate will be in a high-traffic area, such as the walkway leading to a detached garage. A double swinging gate will save time when your arms are full of groceries.

WHERE FENCE MEET: A gate here should be hinged on the side of the section that's nearest the corner of the fence. That way, the

WHERE FENCES MEET

ALONG A SLOPE

swinging gate won't get in the way of views and access through the opening. A two-way gate lends itself well to this kind of opening.

TOP OR BOTTOM OF STAIRS: If the landing is wider than the arc of the gate's swing, you can safely mount a gate at the top or bottom of a flight of stairs. People need enough space to swing the gate, and the landing forewarns that steps exist beyond. In this situation, the gate can swing in one or both directions.

ALONG A SLOPE: If you're building a gate on a slope, hinge it on the low side so that as

the gate swings open, the bottom will clear the slope. Note that the frame is built square, rather than conforming to the angle of the slope. It breaks the visual line of the fence framework, but the gate gets the structural strength it needs. In this situation, the gate can swing in one or both directions.

ACROSS A HILLSIDE: Hills, like slopes, require gates to be hung so they will swing out toward the downhill direction; the bottom of the gate will swing free and clear of the slope of the hillside. Gates hung perpendicular to a hill can swing in one direction only.

ACROSS A HILLSIDE

TOP OR BOTTOM OF STAIRS

DESIGNING GATES: THE DETAILS

Z-FRAME

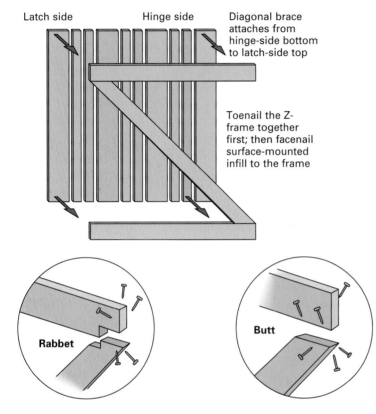

Latch side   Hinge side   Diagonal brace attaches from hinge-side bottom to latch-side top

Toenail the Z-frame together first; then facenail surface-mounted infill to the frame

Rabbet

Butt

CONSTRUCTION TIPS

Use these tips when you build your gate to save time and avoid aggravation later on.

■ Make sure your gate frame stock is equal to its load. You'll find very few gates with frames thinner than 2×4s. But even 2×4s might be too small on a large gate with heavy infill.

■ If you're using panel infill, such as plywood, you won't need a brace. Plywood will keep the gate square.

■ Buy the best wood you can afford. Heartwood of redwood, cypress, or cedar, or pressure-treated lumber are less likely to warp or rot.

■ Make sure all your hardware is rust- and corrosion-resistant—inexpensive hardware will cost you in the long run in added maintenance and gate repair.

■ Do you want to latch your gate open (in addition to being able to latch it closed)? A hook and eye will do the trick. So will a J-latch or cane bolt. They slip into a pipe in the ground.

■ For automatic gate-closing, use a gate spring—one that's strong enough to push the latch closed.

■ To minimize sag on a long gate that swings over a smooth surface, put a wheel near the end of the gate.

Designing and building a gate demand many decisions to be made—but by now you have made most of them.

You have generally (perhaps specifically) chosen the style of your gate and have decided whether it will contrast, complement, or harmonize with the adjacent fence.

You know where the gate will go, how wide it will be, and which way it will swing. You also know if it's a single-panel gate or a pair of panels.

Now it's time to select the framework.

TYPES OF GATE FRAMES

The illustrations at left and on page 79 show the two basic ways to frame a gate—with a Z-frame or a perimeter frame. On the surface and at a quick glance, they may seem to be the same. There are some pertinent differences, however.

■ Z-frames are easier to build because you have fewer joints to make.

■ Either frame design probably holds up equally well under the same conditions, but a Z-frame has less structural strength than a perimeter frame. (Corner or angle brackets will strengthen both styles, especially when built as flat-rail frames.)

■ A perimeter frame can function as a gate even without infill.

■ A Z-frame looks light and casual. A perimeter frame tends to look a little more formal and perhaps even stolid.

■ Both frames can accommodate surface-mounted infill, but only the perimeter frame will accept inset infill. If you plan to install prefabricated lattice panels, plywood, tongue-and-groove siding, or plastic, these materials will look better as inset infill instead of being surface-mounted.

SKETCH YOUR OPTIONS

As you consider which frame to build, make sketches to help determine the one that will fit your fence in a way that best combines style, functionality, and the use it's likely to get. (If you have children who might want to ride the gate, plan to build a strong, reinforced perimeter frame.) If both designs will meet your requirements but the gate will see frequent use, make a perimeter-frame gate. Whatever you choose, keep your sketch handy for use during the next step.

JOINTS AND CLOSURES

Now you're ready to decide which of the joints and what kind of gate stop you'll put on the frame.

PERIMETER FRAME

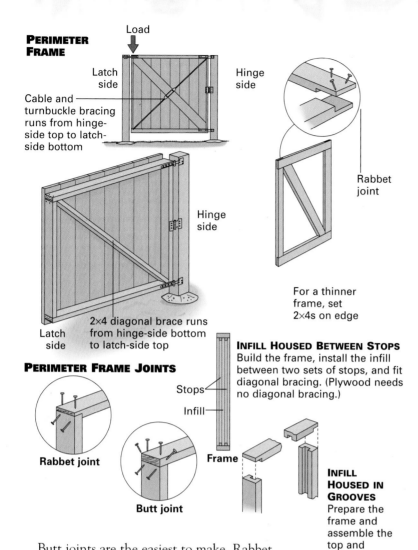

Load

Latch side

Hinge side

Cable and turnbuckle bracing runs from hinge-side top to latch-side bottom

Hinge side

Rabbet joint

For a thinner frame, set 2×4s on edge

Hinge side

Latch side

2×4 diagonal brace runs from hinge-side bottom to latch-side top

PERIMETER FRAME JOINTS

Rabbet joint

Butt joint

Stops

Infill

Frame

INFILL HOUSED BETWEEN STOPS
Build the frame, install the infill between two sets of stops, and fit diagonal bracing. (Plywood needs no diagonal bracing.)

INFILL HOUSED IN GROOVES
Prepare the frame and assemble the top and sides; insert the infill, add the bottom, and fit the bracing

Butt joints are the easiest to make. Rabbet or half-lap joints are stronger.

Gate stops are vertical strips of wood or metal that keep the gate from swinging past the opening. Stops save the hinges from being bent backwards and help the gate to last longer.

Sketching construction details isn't necessary, but sketches with measurements can save a lot of time and frustration when you begin construction. You'll need sketches if you're contracting the work yourself.

JOINTS AND CLOSURES

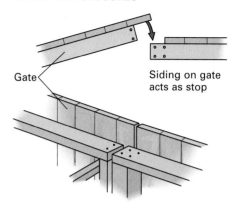

Gate

Siding on gate acts as stop

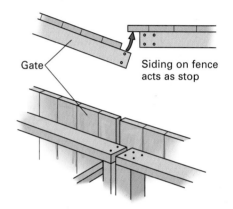

Gate

Siding on fence acts as stop

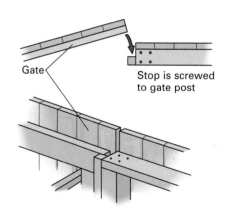

Gate

Stop is screwed to gate post

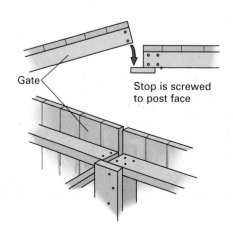

Gate

Stop is screwed to post face

MIX OR MATCH?

Your gate may require a framing style that's different from the fence. While gate frames are usually built in the same style as the fence frame, it's not necessary.

To hang a perimeter-frame gate with flat rails on a fence built with edge-rail construction, minimize the difference in thickness. Do this by placing the gate's hinges so the gate and fence faces are aligned. Conversely, you can build a Z-frame gate with flat rails to match a flat-rail fence. In this case, cut rabbets in the corners, similar to those illustrated on this page, but with the 2×4s mounted flat.

HARDWARE AND HINGES

Attractive gate hardware can improve the looks of a fence. If well designed and fabricated, gate hardware is special and rare. But it's not impossible to find.

Start by looking at the illustrations on this page and the next—these styles are commonly available. Then check with your local building materials supplier and specialty hardware stores. If these don't stock the style you want, there are other sources.

Specialty hardware or restoration catalogues are a good place to look for attractive or unusual hardware. Ornamental iron shops—or even a brass foundry— will make just about anything you want. You'll pay more, of course, but the cost might be worth it for that one-of-a-kind design. Don't forget antique shops and salvage yards. Your own ingenuity at the workbench might produce just the right design.

LATCHES

What do you want in a latch? Ease of operation, security, and suitable style— whether formal or rustic—are the main factors to consider when choosing a latch.

In some cases, the gate size will limit your choice of latches. If the gate is tall, you can't reach over it to get at the latch, for example, so you need one that can be operated from both sides.

For security, some latches include locks or hasps for a padlock. Make sure you can unlock the gate from the inside—a locked gate will interfere with emergency egress and access. Check local codes for requirements that apply to gate exit and entry.

HINGES

Regardless of the style you select, remember that even lightweight gates are heavy, and they're subject to the elements and a lot of wear and tear. Three hinges hang a gate far better than two. Err on the side of excess when you select the hinges and fasteners—make "heavy-duty" and "heavy gauge" your watchwords.

FASTENERS

Screws that fasten your hinges and latches should penetrate the wood frame as deeply as possible without going through the other side.

If the screws supplied with your hinges or latch aren't long enough, to do the job, buy some separately that are. (Get the same gauge screws supplied, but increase their length.) A larger gauge—larger diameter— screw may not fit the holes and countersinks in the hardware. When you buy longer screws, be sure to purchase rustproof ones that will withstand the elements.

CATCHES AND LATCHES

Hook and eye

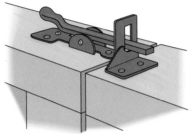

Top latch

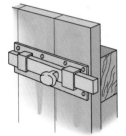

Slide bolt

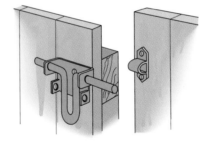

Slide action

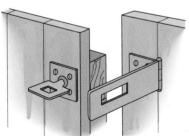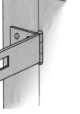

Hasp latch

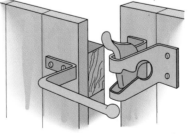

Strike latch

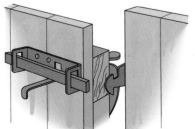

Thumb latch

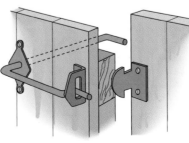

Lever latch

HINGES AND DECORATIVE HARDWARE

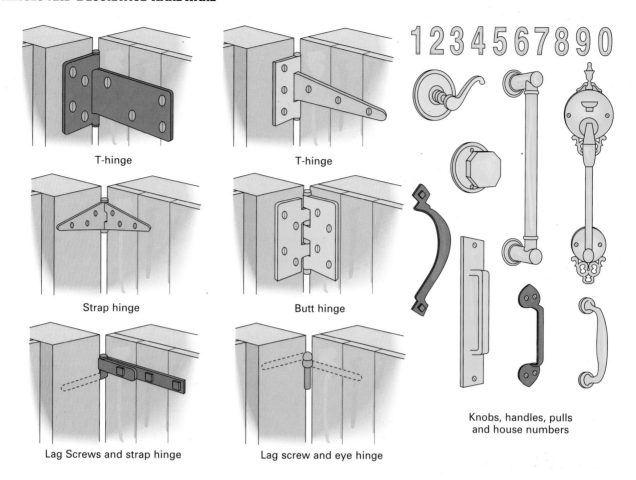

T-hinge

T-hinge

Strap hinge

Butt hinge

Lag Screws and strap hinge

Lag screw and eye hinge

Knobs, handles, pulls
and house numbers

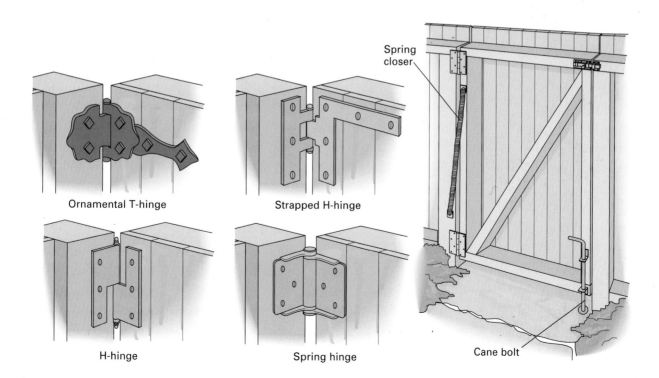

Ornamental T-hinge

Strapped H-hinge

H-hinge

Spring hinge

Spring
closer

Cane bolt

BUILDING AND HANGING A GATE

Gates demand straight and true lumber, so select it carefully. Make the choice yourself. Buy clear, kiln-dried, surfaced lumber to improve the odds that the gate will remain flat and square after continued exposure to the elements.

The illustrations on these two pages show basic construction for a perimeter-frame gate. Follow the same steps for any gate that you build (they apply to all styles).

Gate construction consists of the following seven steps (your own custom design might require additional steps along the way):

MEASURE THE OPENING: Measure the distance between the posts at the bottom of the opening as well as the top. Hold the hinges and latches to the frame when you measure. Cut the outside width of the gate to this measurement, less standard clearances (¼ to ½ inch on the hinge side, ½ to ⅝ inch on the latch side) and whatever additional clearances are required by your hardware.

CUT THE FRAME MEMBERS TO LENGTH: Cut the gate rails to length. If the top and bottom of the gate opening measured differently, the length of the rails should reflect it. Next, cut the stiles to fit between the rails, allowing for the joints you sketched earlier. (Note that when assembled, the rails overlay the stiles so water can't easily enter the joint.)

ASSEMBLE THE FRAME: Working on a flat surface, fasten the frame members together with 3-inch deck screws. (Don't build a gate with nails—they will eventually work their way out.) Use corner or angle brackets to strengthen the assembly.

As you work, make sure that the frame members are flat and square. Use a framing square or measure the diagonals from the outside corners of the cross-members. If the diagonal measurements are the same, the frame is square. (Use this same measuring

MEASURING FOR THE FRAME

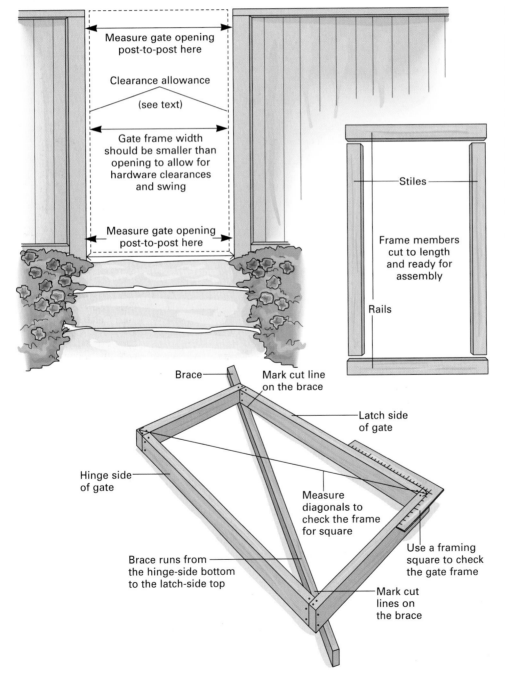

Measure gate opening post-to-post here

Clearance allowance

(see text)

Gate frame width should be smaller than opening to allow for hardware clearances and swing

Measure gate opening post-to-post here

Stiles

Frame members cut to length and ready for assembly

Rails

Brace

Mark cut line on the brace

Latch side of gate

Hinge side of gate

Measure diagonals to check the frame for square

Brace runs from the hinge-side bottom to the latch-side top

Use a framing square to check the gate frame

Mark cut lines on the brace

technique for a Z-frame to make sure that the parts are properly positioned.)

Next, lay the frame down on the bracing member—the piece that runs from the hinge-side bottom to the latch-side top—and mark the cut lines.

When you cut the brace to size, save the line—that is, saw just to the outside of the marks—so the brace will fit tightly. Fasten the brace to the frame with deck screws driven into predrilled holes.

ADD THE INFILL: Lay the frame down with its face up. Make sure the frame is arranged so the brace goes from the hinge-side bottom to the latch-side top. Then fasten the infill with predrilled decking screws, aligning each piece as you go. If you use inset infill, fasten it with stops as you would if hanging inset infill on a fence bay (see page 57).

MOUNT THE HINGES: Measure and mark the hinge positions. Drill pilot holes (make them slightly smaller than the shank of the screw) and fasten the gate leaf of the hinge to the gate. If your gate will close against a wood stop, swing the gate shut. Then, position the stop against the gate and fasten it to the post.

CHECK THE FIT: Gates are heavy and difficult to handle. Fitting them is easier with someone to help. Hold the gate in position (prop it at its proper height on scrap lumber) and see if the clearances and hardware will allow it to open and close freely. If necessary, trim the gate to give it clearance.

HANG THE GATE: With the gate still propped up, wedge shims of the proper clearances along the sides to hold the gate in position while you mark the hardware mounting holes. Mark the position of the hinge mounting hole on the post.

GATE INFILL

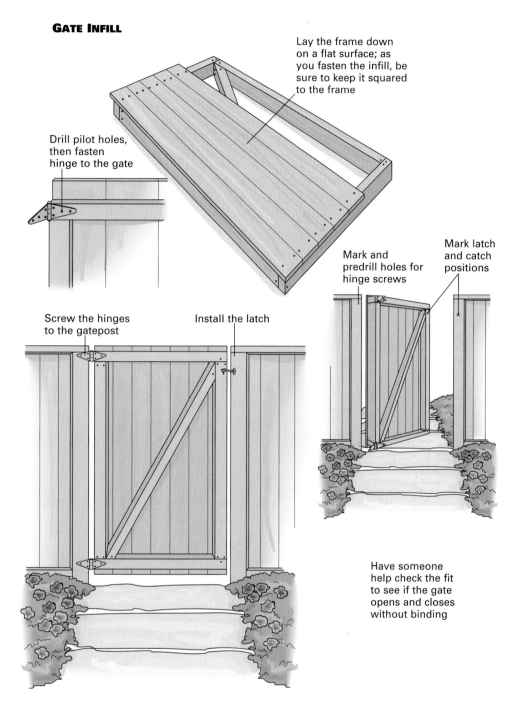

Lay the frame down on a flat surface; as you fasten the infill, be sure to keep it squared to the frame

Drill pilot holes, then fasten hinge to the gate

Mark and predrill holes for hinge screws

Mark latch and catch positions

Screw the hinges to the gatepost

Install the latch

Have someone help check the fit to see if the gate opens and closes without binding

Drill pilot holes and set the hinges. Butt hinges are usually set 4 to 6 inches from the top and bottom. Strap hinges and T-hinges are usually placed on the rails to provide a surface for the screws.

Measure and mark the latch and catch positions, (about 36 inches from the ground, or wherever distance the manufacturer specifies). Mount the hardware on the gate and post.

Finish the gate according to your finish treatment plan. (See page 71 for information about finishes.)

GATE REPAIR

Gates take a lot of abuse. In addition to facing weather extremes, they are pushed, slammed, and sometimes ridden on a regular basis. Fortunately, most gate repairs are not very complicated.

In addition to looking bad, a sagging gate may not open easily or close properly. The cause is usually a loose hinge, an out-of-square gate opening, or an out-of-square gate.

FIXING LOOSE HINGES

If the hinge is loose, your first reaction probably will be to tighten the screws. Loose hinge screws, however, usually indicate that something more than tightening is needed.

As a stop-gap measure, you can install larger or longer screws. Take the old screws to the hardware store and get the next size larger, in a length that will stop just short of going through the other side.

If that doesn't work, you might attach the hinge somewhere else, especially if the hinge was in the wrong place to begin with. But if the hinge is where it should be, it needs to stay there. One solution is to drill through the wood with a bit that just slides through the screw hole in the hinge plate. Then, install the hardware with machine bolts, nuts, and washers, as shown in the illustration above right.

FIXING AN OUT-OF-SQUARE GATE OPENING

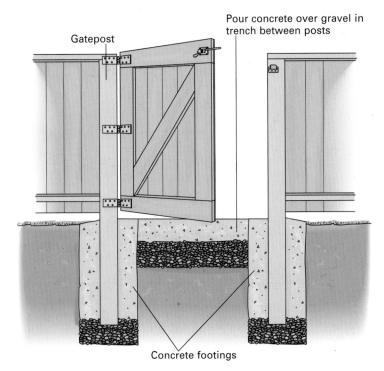

Gatepost

Pour concrete over gravel in trench between posts

Concrete footings

WASHERS AND NUTS

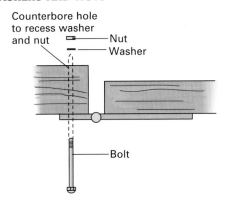

Counterbore hole to recess washer and nut

Nut

Washer

Bolt

When the drill bit just breaks through the opposite side, drill a counterbore around the hole for the nut and washer. Insert a bolt with a length equal to the thickness of the stock you've just drilled. That way, you won't have too much of the bolt extending so things catch on it.

For a more permanent repair, remove the hinge, then drill out the holes to the correct diameter for a length of dowel. (Usually a ⅜-inch dowel is sufficient; buy the dowel before drilling the holes, though. Many ⅜-inch dowels are not actually ⅜ inch in diameter.) Plug the holes with wood dowels thinly coated with waterproof glue. Let the dowels extend slightly from the holes.

Let the glue dry, then shave the dowels flush to the surface with a chisel. Drill pilot holes into the dowels, and reattach the hinge by driving screws into the dowels. Use the largest and longest screws possible.

This method will repair worn lag screw holes as well, but for lag screw hinges, drill out the post for a ½- or ⅝-inch dowel.

A loose hinge problem may not originate with the fastener at all. The hinge may be loose because it's carrying more than its designed weight. (Gates higher than 5 feet or wider than 3 feet need three hinges). The solution is to add a hinge of the same strength or install 3 new and heavier models.

As a last resort, check the way the hinges seat against the gate or post. Inset hinges may not be shimmed properly. If the hinges sit in mortises unevenly, put shims behind them and reset the screws through the shims.

OPENING OUT OF SQUARE

If the gate opening is out of square (measure at the top and bottom to find out), the problem is probably loose gateposts. If both

REPAIRING LOOSE SCREW HOLES WITH DOWELS

Dowel

Waterproof glue

gateposts are loose, here's how to remedy the situation by tying them together with a concrete trench.

First, take the gate off and dig a trench between the posts—as wide as the post footings. If the posts are not set in concrete, brace them on both sides and dig around them also, to half their depth. If the posts have concrete footings, excavate to two-thirds of their depth on the side opposite the direction they're leaning

Line the bottom of your trench (and post holes without concrete) with 3 inches of gravel. Pull the posts back into plumb with a come-along anchored at one end with a rod driven into the soil (see page 69). Then backfill the excavation with concrete until it's full. The concrete will form a collar around the posts. Slope the surface to let rainwater drain off. Keep the posts braced plumb until the concrete cures.

If the unsquare opening is caused by a leaning post (most likely the hinge post), brace the post and dig out the footing (break up concrete with a sledge and pick). Plumb the post and reset it, keeping the braces in place until the concrete cures (three to seven days).

You may also be able to true an errant post with a turnbuckle. Fasten one end of the turnbuckle to the top of the gate post and the other end to the bottom of the next post. Tighten the turnbuckle to pull the post into plumb.

GATE OUT OF SQUARE

An out-of-square gate will often respond to a turnbuckle also. Attach the turnbuckle as shown below, from the top hinge-side corner to the lower latch-side corner. It won't be effective if you attach it the other way. Tighten the turnbuckle until the gate is square.

You can also remove the gate, square it up and install additional supports (corner brackets, angle brackets, or triangular wooden gussets). If your gate was constructed without a diagonal support and you add one, install it from the upper latch-side corner to the lower hinge-side corner—just the opposite of the way you attach a turnbuckle.

BINDING GATE

The weather can affect the movement of a gate. If the gate binds after a rain but swings freely when it's dry, it could use a little planing. You can find out where it's binding when it's wet (mark the spot), but don't plane it until the wood is dry. Planing wet wood will leave you with a clogged plane at best and a scarred surface at worst.

You may also be able to tell where it's binding even if it's dry. Check the gate clearance. If any area is less than ¼ inch, that's probably where the gate is binding when it swells up from moisture.

Sometimes latches will catch only in wet weather. If this is the problem with your gate, relocate the latch or install one that has a longer reach.

USING A TURNBUCKLE

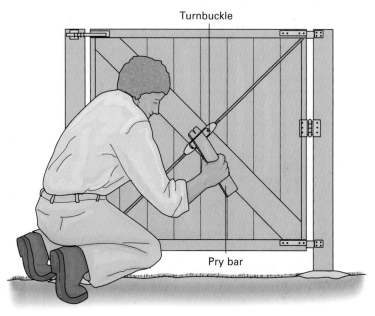

Turnbuckle

Pry bar

TOOLS AND MATERIALS

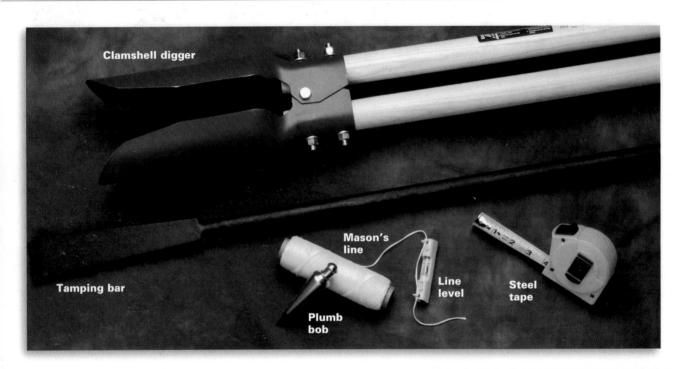

Clamshell digger

Tamping bar

Mason's line

Plumb bob

Line level

Steel tape

Building fences requires a modest collection of tools and some knowledge of lumber and other materials and fasteners. You'll find that information in this chapter.

Tools fall into three categories: Layout, digging, and building tools. You may already own most of the tools you'll need for fence-building. You can rent or buy most of the others. When you need a tool, a good approach is to buy the tools you think you'll have future use for and rent those you'll use infrequently. When you purchase tools, always buy the best quality you can afford.

Lumber and other fencing materials are widely available at lumberyards and home centers. When shopping for materials, remember that more-costly treated lumber, cedar, and redwood will also last longer. Consider maintenance as well as current cost.

LAYOUT TOOLS

Although fence layout can be the most exacting aspect of fence building, layout tools need not be expensive. An inexpensive tape measure will measure as accurately as one that costs twice as much.
Here's what you'll need.
LINE LEVEL: This small level has a hook on each end so it can hang on lines stretched over distances too long to level with a carpenter's level.
MASON'S LINE: This is the mainstay of layout work. Use nylon; it doesn't stretch.
STEEL TAPE: This is a do-it-yourselfer's constant companion. A 1-inch blade will extend farther without sagging. You'll need a 16-footer—a 25-foot one if your fence is long.
PLUMB BOB: This makes quick work of marking post hole locations so you can dig them in the right place.

DIGGING TOOLS

Although there are only two tools in this category, rent or buy high-quality ones—you don't want any breakdowns.

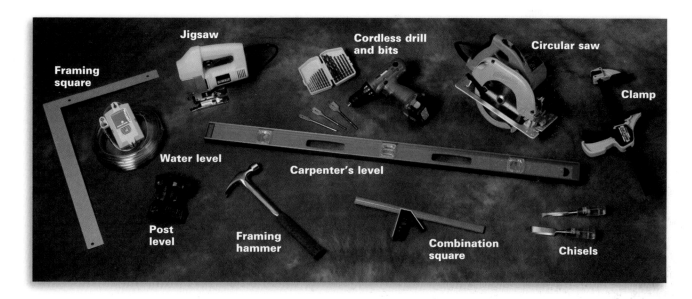

CLAMSHELL DIGGER: Its hinged shovels will dig clean, straight-sided postholes in almost any soil.

TAMPING BAR: You'll need this to remove rocks that nature put where you want to dig postholes. Tamp the fill with a 2x4.

FENCE-BUILDING TOOLS

These tools are the backbone of do-it-yourself carpentry. If you're assembling your tool chest for the first time, buy good tools. You'll use them for other projects, many of which won't occur to you until you own the tools.

CARPENTER'S LEVEL: A 48-inch model will plumb posts and infill. Shorter versions may give false readings—which you discover only after you step back from a completed bay. Buy one with a stiff steel frame.

FRAMING SQUARE: You'll use this for quick, preliminary checks for right angles.

CIRCULAR SAW: These come in different sizes. Get a model with a 7¼-inch blade and a heavy-duty motor. The extra power and durability are valuable in fence building or any other project that requires cutting through posts or framing members. Buy a carbide-tipped combination blade.

JIGSAW: If you're cutting any fancy patterns, you'll need one of these. (Buy a heavy-duty model here, too.)

CORDLESS DRILL: This is an essential tool. It drills holes and makes driving screws a snap. Buy a 12- or 14.4-volt model. You'll need spade bits of appropriate sizes for larger holes and to start mortises. Twist drills will take care of holes for screws and bolts.

FRAMING HAMMER: Buy a high-quality hammer. A 20-ounce hammer is better than a 16-ounce one for fences. The extra weight may be tiring at first, but you'll be thankful for it after driving a fenceful of 10d nails.

POST LEVEL: This is a one-purpose tool, but nothing does it better. Strap it to a post to plumb two sides at once.

WATER LEVEL: This device attaches to the ends of your garden hose. Filled with water, it makes long-distance leveling easy.

CHISELS: You'll need chisels to shape mortises and tenons. Buy high-quality chisels and take good care of them. Drive chisels with a mallet, not a metal hammer. Sharp chisels make clean, accurate cuts easily. (Poor-fitting mortises make weak joints.)

COMBINATION SQUARE: This is an indispensable tool. It helps you check 90- and 45-degree angles quickly, measure depth from surfaces, and lay out cutting lines.

SAFETY FIRST

Don't let pain or injury mar your project. Avoid accidents by following some standard safety precautions.

■ Wear safety glasses when hammering, sawing, or doing any other task that might send something into your eyes.

■ Always keep your eyes on your work— especially when using any power tool.

■ Don't wear sneakers—wear hard-soled work boots. Those with steel toes are safest.

■ Wear a dust mask when sawing or doing anything that raises dust.

■ Wear knee pads when kneeling.

■ Don't wear loose-fitting clothes that could trip you or get caught in machinery.

■ Don't leave tools on top of a stepladder. You'll regret it when you move the ladder.

■ Know your limitations. Take regular breaks, even if you don't feel tired.

LUMBER BASICS

Your choice of wood will affect the cost of your fence, its appearance, and how long it will last. Although the process of picking the right materials might seem daunting—with so many species and lumber grades—there are just a few criteria you need to keep in mind. Appearance, cost, and durability should rank high on your list of lumber selection "rules."

RESISTANT WOODS

You can count on the appearance and durability of these naturally rot-resistant species for fence work. These woods are more expensive than others (redwood is the most costly) and their cost (as well as that of any species) rises the farther you live from their natural growth area.

REDWOOD: One of the species most commonly used as untreated lumber, redwood has a close grain and is naturally resistant to weathering, warping, cupping, and shrinkage. Its more than 30 grades are based on appearance and color as well as strength. Only the heartwood (a deep reddish brown) is decay-resistant. Stained, redwood finishes to a rich color. Untreated, it weathers to a beautiful silvery gray.

CEDAR: Natural beauty and resistance to decay and insects characterize cedar. You'll often see it in split-rail fencing. Cedar works easily, although it's much more likely to split than other woods. Left untreated, it weathers to a fine gray like redwood.

CYPRESS: Cypress grows in swampy areas of the South, a reason for its natural resistance to rot and decay. It also weathers to a silvery gray. Cypress stock may be hard to find outside its natural growth areas.

The resistant woods are assigned to one of several grades, but only their heartwood is naturally resistant to weathering. Use heartwood for posts and kickboards. Use sapwood treated with a sealer for rails and infill only if it will be dry for most of the year.

FIR AND PINE

These species are strong, lightweight, widely available, and less expensive than naturally resistant woods. They come in two forms:

■ **UNTREATED LUMBER:** Commonly used for batterboards and disposable bracing. It won't withstand the outdoor elements if unfinished. It's not suitable for posts at all, but can be used for rails and infill if painted.

■ **PRESSURE-TREATED LUMBER:** A less expensive substitute for redwood, cedar, and cypress, pressure-treated lumber is extremely rot-resistant (see page 89).

LUMBER GRADES

Lumber is divided into categories according to its thickness. *Boards* are less than 2 inches thick, and *dimension lumber* is 2 to 4 inches thick. Lumber is graded for its strength and appearance following standards established by independent agencies.

BOARDS: Fir and pine boards are graded in two categories—select and common.

■ **SELECT:** This is the best stock—with either few or no knots—for fine finishwork. Here are the four grades of select boards:

  A: contains no knots
  B: has only small blemishes
  C: has some minor defects, small knots, and blemishes
  D: has larger blemishes that can be concealed with paint

■ **COMMON:** Utility grades ranked from 1 to 5 in descending quality. A middle grade, such as no. 3, is a good choice for many projects.

DIMENSION LUMBER: Fir and pine dimension lumber grades are:

Lumber for fencing comes in several species and a number of styles. For the framework, 4×4 posts and 2×4 rails are standard. Board infill is often available with decoratively cut ends and in varying widths.

- **CONSTRUCTION GRADE:** top of the line
- **STANDARD GRADE:** almost as good, but cheaper than construction grade
- **UTILITY GRADE:** low quality stock, unsuitable for framing

Pressure-treated lumber also comes in a variety of grades, from those treated for ground-contact for posts and retaining walls, to lighter treatments for fences or deck boards. Redwood lumber is classified as garden grades or architectural grades.

You should buy standard-grade dimensional lumber and common-grade no. 3 boards— or better—if you can afford it. Look at the chart on page 92 for a comparison of material costs and other factors.

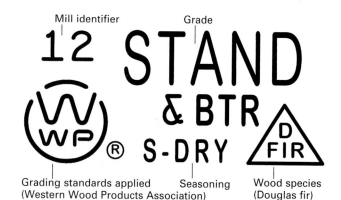

Mill identifier — Grade

Grading standards applied (Western Wood Products Association) — Seasoning — Wood species (Douglas fir)

GRADE STAMPS

Grade stamps show the lumber species, the prevalence of defects, quality, and moisture content. A grade stamp may also have a number or the name of the mill that produced it, and have a certification symbol that shows the lumber association that has issued the grading standards.

Pressure-treated lumber will also list the year it was treated, the chemical used as a preservative, a unit of measure called the exposure condition (whether it can be used for ground contact or is suitable only for aboveground installation), and the amount of chemical used to treat it.

SEASONING

Most lumber is either air-dried or kiln-dried before sale. One of three marks will specify moisture content of fir and pine at the time the lumber was surfaced: S-GRN (green lumber), over 19 percent; S-DRY, up to 19 percent; MC 15, up to 15 percent.

Dry lumber (S-DRY or MC 15) is less likely to warp, works more easily, holds fasteners more tightly, and finishes better.

PRESSURE-TREATED LUMBER

Wood is often treated with various chemicals to improve its rot resistance. Those chemicals (along with other information) are identified on grade stamps on pressure-treated lumber.

Chromated copper arsenate (CCA) is the most widely used, often on southern yellow pine. You can identify it easily by its green tinge. Ammoniacal copper arsenate (ACA) is used to treat Douglas fir and other hard-to-treat species. Ammoniacal copper quaternary ammonia (ACQ) is a new preservative. It contains no hazardous ingredients.

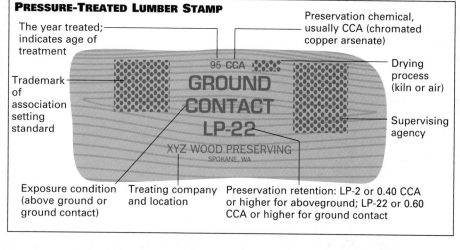

PRESSURE-TREATED LUMBER STAMP

The year treated; indicates age of treatment

Preservation chemical, usually CCA (chromated copper arsenate)

Trademark of association setting standard

Drying process (kiln or air)

95 CCA
GROUND CONTACT LP-22
XYZ WOOD PRESERVING
SPOKANE, WA

Supervising agency

Exposure condition (above ground or ground contact)

Treating company and location

Preservation retention: LP-2 or 0.40 CCA or higher for aboveground; LP-22 or 0.60 CCA or higher for ground contact

The stamp on pressure-treated lumber also identifies its retention level—a measure of how much preservative the lumber holds. Posts and any other pieces that are in contact with the ground or that are likely to stay wet should be marked for ground contact. Other fence components, such as pickets and infill, can be built with lumber treated to above-ground standards.

Pressure treatment is not a substitute for finishing the wood. A couple of weeks after construction, apply water-repellent sealer—several coats on cut ends. After it dries for two to three months, apply paint or stain. You'll need to refinish pressure-treated stock from time to time. An unfinished fence built with treated wood will gradually turn a pleasant, weathered gray; but if it remains unfinished, it may not last long.

LUMBER BASICS
continued

This is your best choice for fence and gate frames, infill, and trimwork. Green lumber produces a rustic look.

PLYWOOD

Manufacturers produce plywood (a sheet material made from thin layers of wood that are glued together for strength) in a variety of sizes, thicknesses, textures, species, and grades. Any plywood used for outdoor construction must be an exterior-grade material—made with glues that will not deteriorate when exposed to moisture—so that the veneers will stay tightly bonded and the sheet will stay flat.

Purchase AA exterior grades (see box at bottom of page 91) for sheathing that you will stain or paint or that will be visible from both sides. Lesser grades have blemishes that will show through the finish but will work just fine for sheathing covered with another material, such as shingles.

The plywood grade stamp will give you most of the information you need to make purchases. It shows whether the wood is suitable for ground contact or above-ground use, whether it can be used as sheathing, its thickness, and the distance it can span over rafters and joists.

Plywood is stiff and rigid, so it doesn't absorb or filter winds. That's why it should be supported on a framework that's strong enough to support not only its weight, but also the lateral forces of wind shear.

WOOD SURFACES

Closely examine the surface of your lumber before buying it. Surfacing affects the fence's final appearance and its ability to take finishes. Rough-sawn lumber may be just perfect of a rustic look. Other styles will look better with stock that is finished (dressed) and planed smooth on one or more sides.

Framing lumber and pressure-treated stock are usually finished on all four sides (S4S). If you want a smooth surface or you plan to paint it, use S4S lumber for posts and rails.

Rough sawn lumber has splinters on its surface. It costs less than dressed lumber but soaks up paints and stains at about twice the rate of finished surfaces.

LOOK BEFORE BUYING

To get a sense of the materials that are right for your fence project, go exploring through a lumberyard.

Look at the different species and examine their colors and grain patterns. Assess quality differences between the grades. See how rough-sawn material is different in appearance and size from surfaced lumber.

Compare pressure-treated with untreated wood. If you don't have a good idea of what you'd like to use, take your fence-line layout and elevation sketch with you and ask a salesperson to recommend wood and make a cost estimate. Then take a second look.

Go through the lumber racks and check for defects. Sight down the length of boards on the flat side and at the edge. Are they crooked or warped? Or are they square and flat? Check for knots. Are they small or tight?

LUMBER DEFECTS

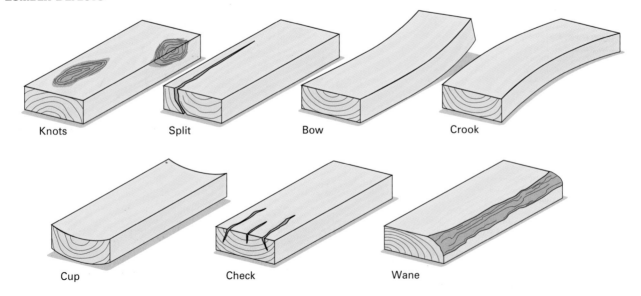

Knots   Split   Bow   Crook

Cup   Check   Wane

Loose and large? Look for checks and splits. If the wood hasn't been kiln-dried, you can expect that more checks and splits will develop as the lumber seasons.

When you have answers to the basic questions and have a good idea about the material you want to use, shop around to compare costs. You might find that a higher-grade material costs less at one yard than does a lower-grade material at another yard.

NOMINAL VERSUS ACTUAL

The dimensions used to describe the size of lumber—1×4, 2×4, 2×6, and so forth—are its nominal dimensions. They specify the size to which the stock was originally cut. That size shrinks when the material is surfaced. For example, the actual size of a surfaced 1×4 is ¾ inch by 3½ inches; a 2×4 measures 1½ by 3½ inches.

Reductions in size from nominal to actual dimensions are about the same from one kind of lumber to another, although pressure-treated boards may vary slightly from untreated boards. If size is particularly significant to your design, measure the actual dimensions. For example, if you want an infill of spaced, rough-sawn, 1×6 boards that is inset between posts, you'll need to know how many boards and spaces will fit in a bay.

ESTIMATING, ORDERING, AND STORING

You can quickly get an idea of costs by visiting your lumberyard and asking the salesperson to give you the materials cost for the basic style of fence you want. Don't hesitate to ask for estimates from several suppliers. Compare costs as well as service.

Ordering lumber requires more attention to detail. You'll need to supply specific information about the quantity of each size of lumber, the species you want, what kind

LUMBER: WHAT SIZE IS IT REALLY?

After it is cut, lumber is dried, planed, and smoothed, reducing its thickness and width. Nominal size refers to the size before drying and planing; actual size is the size you actually get from the lumberyard.

Nominal Size	Actual Size
1×2	¾" × 1½"
1×3	¾" × 2¼"
1×4	¾" × 3½"
1×6	¾" × 5½"
1×8	¾" × 7¼"
1×10	¾" × 9¼"
1×12	¾" × 11¼"
2×2	1½" × 1½"
2×4	1½" × 3½"
2×6	1½" × 5½"
2×8	1½" × 7¼"
2×10	1½" × 9¼"
2×12	1½" × 11¼"

of footings you'll be pouring, and how you will finish the fence. You might be able to negotiate a better price for materials if you place the full order with one supplier. Don't forget to include delivery costs in your estimate, especially if you're building a long fence or don't own a truck.

When your materials arrive, protect them from direct sunlight and moisture. If it has not been kiln-dried, let it dry for several weeks. Stack the boards so that they are flat and evenly weighted, inserting spacers (called "stickers") between them. Store them under a cover or in the shade. Kiln-dried lumber should be dry enough to use right away, but it, too, needs to be protected from rain and direct sunlight before construction begins.

PLYWOOD GRADES

Grade	Description
AA	Good on both sides. Highest quality, with no knots, defects, or voids. Readily accepts stains and paint. This is the material to get if both sides of panel fencing is visible.
AB	Good on one side (no knots or holes). The reverse side is smooth but has some defects. It may have patched "football" areas where large knots used to be. There are few voids in the interior. It can be sanded and painted for fences that have both sides visible.
AC	Good on one side. The other side has knots, minor defects, and "footballs." The interior has some small voids. It's suitable for fences that have only one side visible.
BB	Both sides have defects, but most of them can be sanded smooth or patched for painting. Usable for fencing where one side is visible (but not without major effort) or as sheathing covered by clapboard, shingles, or other material.

OTHER MATERIALS

VINYL FENCING

Vinyl fencing, made of the same polyvinyl chloride (PVC) as siding and plumbing pipe, comes in a variety of styles that resemble wood and metal varieties. You can get vinyl pickets, lattice, boards—even vinyl basket weave. It comes in prefabricated panels (some require assembly). A few styles are designed to follow the contour of a slope, and you can modify end posts to install stepped styles.

Although its lateral and load-bearing strength is not as great as wood or metal, it is otherwise virtually indestructible. Vinyl fencing comes in colors (typically whites and browns), doesn't need painting (ever!), and won't peel, rust, or decay.

Most models are made as kits with posts, rails, and infill cut to the right lengths. Panels are usually 72 to 96 inches long.

PREFABRICATED WOOD PANELS

Prefabricated wood-fence panels are made for fence builders in a hurry. They are usually available in 6- and 8-foot lengths. All you have to do is install posts, nail on the bays, and apply the finish. You may even find that it is less expensive to buy prefabricated bays than to build your own.

Before you decide to use prefabricated bays, examine them carefully. They are available in a wide variety of styles, prices, grades— and quality. Lower cost may mean shortcuts have been taken in quality of materials or construction or both.

Buy panels made with pressure-treated lumber and 2×4 rails. They should be assembled with galvanized nails (not staples). Make sure the product is a worthwhile investment that will give you years of service and not require excessive maintenance.

TUBULAR METAL

Tubular aluminum and steel fences are manufactured in a wide variety of sizes, designs, and colors. Kits usually come complete with posts, rails, prefabricated panels (in 72- to 96-inch lengths and various heights), and the hardware needed to fasten the parts together.

If you're fencing on a moderate slope, use a style with a frame you can rack to match the angle of the ground. Steep slopes will require angled panels. Stepped fencing must be custom made.

You'll find prepainted metal fencing in black, white, or brown (make sure the finish is a poly powder coating). If you buy unpainted fencing, apply a high-quality, rust-resistant paint before you put up the fence.

Most tubular fence designs attach to metal posts that are set in concrete. Some prefab panels, however, attach to wooden posts or masonry columns with special brackets. What is consistent among all tubular fence designs is the necessity to install them one panel (and one post) at a time.

These fences require careful planning, but assembly is easy. Most suppliers will build the fence for an additional fee.

MATERIALS COMPARISON

Choosing materials is a balancing act. Listed below are some of the factors to consider. They are ranked on a scale of 1 (least or shortest) to 5 (most or longest). The rankings are generalized because local costs may vary, and climate may affect the life of the material and the maintenance required.

Material	Cost	Maintenance	Life Expectancy
WOOD			
Redwood	5	2	4
Cedar, cypress	4	2	4
Pressure-treated	2-3	3-4	3
Prefab panels	2-3	3-5	2-3
OTHER			
Wrought iron	5	4	5
Steel, aluminum	3-4	2	4-5
Chain link	3	1	4
Wire mesh	2-3	3-4	3
Vinyl	2-3	1	5

FASTENERS

An old saying in the carpentry trade is "Fasteners are the first to go." Don't scrimp on quality or quantity when selecting the fasteners—they're supposed to hold all your hard work together.

Nails are the least expensive fastener for most fences. Screws cost more, but they make a stronger joint and, ultimately, that means a longer-lasting fence. Although driving an individual screw takes slightly longer than pounding a nail, screws can save you time in the long run. If you brace your posts solidly, you can begin building your fence with screws as soon as the concrete sets; you don't have to wait for it to cure.

NAILS

The metal used to make nails makes a difference. Some nails rust easily, and others won't ever rust. Rust leaves dark stains on the fence surface that bleed through paint, and weaken the nail, which can ultimately weaken the fence. If you're nailing, choose one of these three types:

■ Hot-dipped galvanized (HDG) nails reduce (but don't eliminate) chances of rusting.

■ Aluminum nails won't rust, but they aren't quite as strong as HDG nails and they can be very difficult to drive (they bend), especially in hard types of woods.

■ Stainless-steel nails won't rust, but they are very expensive, and not all materials suppliers stock them. They're a good choice for fences built near salt water.

Another difference relates to the nail shank. Nail shanks have different holding power. Ring-shank and spiral-shank nails grip the wood fibers better than smooth (common or box) nails, and don't easily work their way out. In fact, they can be difficult to remove.

Although there is a wide selection of nail sizes and shapes available, these nails work well for most fence projects.

■ Common or ring-shank nails (16d) for the frame—in 2× or thicker stock

■ Box or ring-shank nails (8d or 10d) for the infill—in 1× or thinner stock

■ Finish nails (6d or 8d) for the fine trim

■ Duplex nails as temporary fasteners; they have a double head, which makes them easy to pull out when you strip away forms or braces, for example

SCREWS

Screws hold better than nails and also come in a number of styles. Fence construction requires deck screws—usually in 2½- to 3½-inch lengths. Deck screws are coated to resist the elements, and are sharp, tapered, and self-

FASTENERS

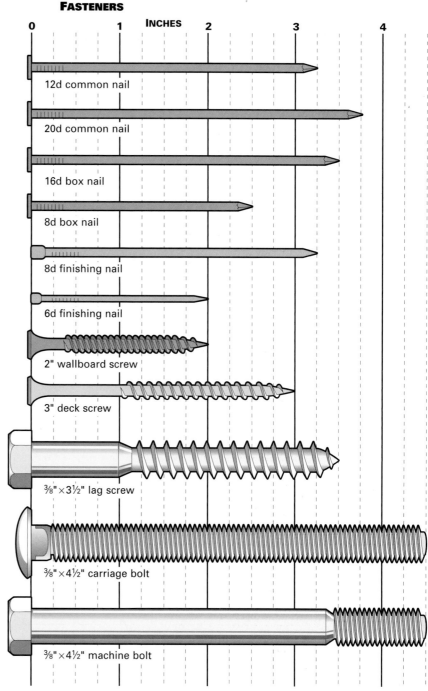

INCHES

0   1   2   3   4

12d common nail

20d common nail

16d box nail

8d box nail

8d finishing nail

6d finishing nail

2" wallboard screw

3" deck screw

⅜" × 3½" lag screw

⅜" × 4½" carriage bolt

⅜" × 4½" machine bolt

FASTENERS
continued

METAL BRACKETS

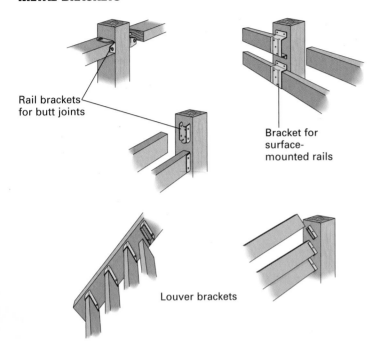

Rail brackets for butt joints

Bracket for surface-mounted rails

Louver brackets

DRILLING PILOT HOLES FOR DECK SCREWS IN SOFTWOOD

Drill through the top piece and into the bottom piece to a depth equal to the screw length. Clamp or hold the parts together as you drive in the screw.

Screw Diameter	Pilot Hole Diameter
4	$\frac{1}{16}$"
6	$\frac{3}{32}$"
8	$\frac{7}{64}$"
10	$\frac{1}{8}$"
12	$\frac{9}{64}$"
14	$\frac{5}{32}$"

BOLTS AND BRACKETS

Bolts, nuts, and washers provide a solid connection with excellent load-bearing strength. Use only zinc-coated or stainless-steel ones. Drill holes with a bit of the same diameter.

Metal fence brackets work well for quick installations and solid connections. Brackets can join rails to posts, prefabricated fence bays to posts, and louvered boards to posts (horizontal louvers) or rails (vertical louvers).

GET A GRIP

Whether you assemble your fence with nails or screws, make sure that two-thirds of the fastener shank is in the lower (usually the thicker) member of the joint. Where possible, and to get the best holding power, drive the fasteners at an angle, toward or away from each other.

sinking. You can drive them with a cordless drill about as quickly as you can hammer nails.

Regardless of the size you use, predrill holes for them (see the chart, above right) when driving them within 2 inches of the end of a board. This keeps the wood from splitting.

A lag screw is a bolt in a screw's clothing—its large size will secure heavy framing members and hardware. Lag screws have a hex-head (square heads are available but uncommon). Tighten them with a wrench.

MIXING CONCRETE

Mixing concrete for post holes is usually easier with premixed bags. All the ingredients are measured—you just have to add the water and the muscle power to mix it. Premix is slightly more costly than mixing your own concrete from dry materials, but the expense is more than offset by the convenience.

How many sacks of premix do you need? Holes for 4×4 posts (3 feet deep) require only a little more than

2 cubic feet each (hardly any at all, in terms of the concrete). Estimate two 60-pound sacks per posthole. (You can fill about three postholes with four 90-pound sacks of premix.)

Pour the concrete into one end of a wheelbarrow, add water a little at a time, then stir the mix into the liquid. Keep the mix somewhat stiff so the soil won't work its way into it. It's ready when it stays in a ball you can form in your hand.

You can mix your own with 1 part portland cement, 1 part sand, and $1\frac{1}{2}$ parts gravel. Measure shovelfuls of dry ingredients into a wheelbarrow or mortar box, or pile them on a piece of plywood. Mix the sand and cement first, then add the gravel and mix again. Hollow out the center of the mix and add a little water. Pull the dry ingredients into the center a little at a time, adding water until the mix is stiff.